THE
CHANGING
SUPREME
COURT

THE
CHANGING
SUPREME
COURT

**EDMUND
LINDOP**

DEMOCRACY IN ACTION

FRANKLIN WATTS
A Division of Grolier Publishing
New York / London / Hong Kong / Sydney
Danbury, Connecticut

Frontispiece: The Supreme Court stands as a monument to the nation's commitment to "Equal Justice Under Law."

*To Jane and Howard Davis,
whose friendship and encouragement
are a constant source of inspiration*

Photographs copyright ©:
The Collection of the Supreme Court of the United States: pp. 2
(Franz Jantzen), 49 (Hessler Studios), 66, 110, 134, 138
(National Geographic Society), 154; UPI/Bettmann: pp. 21, 35, 39, 51, 118;
Wide World Photos: pp. 46, 94; Jay Mallin: p. 75;
Reuters/Bettmann: p. 83; The Bettmann Archive: p.99.

Library of Congress Cataloging-in-Publication Data

Lindop, Edmund.
The Changing Supreme Court/by Edmund Lindop.
p. cm.—(Democracy in action)
Includes bibliographical references and index.
ISBN 0-531-11224-1
1. United States—Constitutional history—Juvenile literature.
2. Judicial review—United States—History—Juvenile literature.
3. United States. Supreme Court—History—Juvenile literature.
[1. United States. Supreme Court—History. 2. United States—
Constitutional history.] I. Title. II. Series: Democracy in
action (Franklin Watts, Inc.)
KF4541.Z9L562 1995
347.73'26'09—dc20
[347.3073509] 95-13842
CIP AC

CONTENTS

CHAPTER ONE

THE HIGHEST COURT IN THE LAND

T he Supreme Court is the most powerful court of law in the United States. Article III, Section 1, of the Constitution provides that "the judicial power of the United States shall be vested in one Supreme Court, and in such inferior courts as the Congress may from time to time ordain and establish."

At the time that the Constitution was written, in 1787, the courts in most countries were part of the government's executive department. But the Founding Fathers who drew up the Constitution were determined that no part of the new national, or federal, government would have sufficient power to oppress the people. So they divided the federal government into three branches: legislative (Congress), executive (headed by the president), and judicial (federal courts).

The Judiciary Act passed by Congress in 1789 provided for a Supreme Court consisting of one chief justice and five associate justices. The number of justices was increased by Congress to seven in 1807, to nine in 1837, and to ten in 1863. Three years later the Court's membership was decreased to seven. But in 1869 the number of justices was increased again to nine, where it has remained to the present.

The Constitution is the supreme law of the land, and the Supreme Court is the guardian of the Constitution. It possesses the power of *judicial review,* which is the authority to strike down any act of government (federal, state, or local) that the justices decide violates the Constitution. This authority was not mentioned in the Constitution, but it was first asserted by Chief Justice John Marshall in the case of *Marbury* v. *Madison* in 1803. Ever since then, judicial review has continued to be the Supreme Court's most important function.

Supreme Court justices are appointed by the president, but the Senate has the power to confirm (approve) or reject the president's nominees. A majority vote of the Senate is required to confirm an appointment to the Court. Unlike presidents and members of Congress, justices may remain in office for life, or until they resign or retire. They have life terms so that they can be independent. In this way, they can make judgments and render decisions without fear of being pressured by political parties or other partisan groups. A Supreme Court justice can be removed only through impeachment for corruption or other abuses of office, but that has never occurred.

The federal judiciary consists of many courts besides the Supreme Court. The most numerous are the federal district courts at the local level. In 1891, Congress passed the Circuit Court of Appeals Act, establishing eleven intermediate circuit courts that hear appeals from the federal district courts. These appellate courts are located in the different regions of the United States, and each of them reviews contested lower-court decisions in its region. Just as the federal government has its judiciary, so does every state. Each separate state court system includes its own supreme court. But all American courts, whether federal or state, are inferior to the United States Supreme Court. Its decisions can be overturned only by new amendments to the Constitution, by the Supreme Court itself, or by acts of Congress. (Since 1975, Congress has overturned about six Supreme Court decisions each year.)

The Constitution gives the Supreme Court two types of authority: *original jurisdiction* and *appellate jurisdiction.* (Jurisdiction is the authority to interpret and apply laws.) Original jurisdiction refers to cases tried before the Supreme Court without involving lower courts. The chief areas in which the High Court has original jurisdiction are legal disputes between two or more states, between the national government and one or more states, and between foreigners and either the United States or a state.

Most of the work of the Supreme Court stems from its appellate jurisdiction, which is its authority to uphold or reverse decisions of lower courts. The cases reviewed by the Supreme Court generally come from the federal courts of appeals or the state supreme courts.

Cases usually reach the Supreme Court in one of two ways: by appeals or by *certiorari*. Appeals cases are those that challenge a federal law, a state law, or a local statute as being inconsistent with the Constitution, or unconstitutional. (A law that is found unconstitutional is declared null and void and cannot be enforced.) Certiorari cases are reviews of lower-court decisions. Generally one of the parties in such a case contends that a serious error was made by a lower court. Every year the Supreme Court receives thousands of petitions to review decisions. Since it cannot possibly review all these cases, the Court generally selects ones that it considers especially important and that involve a significant public interest. A certiorari case is generally accepted if four justices agree that it merits review.

THE SUPREME COURT IN ACTION

Yearly sessions of the Supreme Court begin in early October and continue until about the end of June. Since 1935, the High Court has conducted its business in a handsome white-marble building in Washington, D.C. Inscribed above the building's entrance is the Court motto: "Equal justice under law."

When the Supreme Court agrees to consider a case tried in a lower court, it does not summon the witnesses who testified in the trial. Instead, it hears arguments from attorneys representing both sides. During the oral arguments, the justices may interrupt and ask questions. The attorneys for each side also present a written argument and summary called a *brief*.

After the justices have considered both the oral and written arguments, they meet in a private conference to discuss the case.

At the end of the conference, the justices generally vote on the case in reverse order of seniority. This may be only a preliminary, informal vote, since some justices may require additional time before making a final judgment. When the formal vote is finally taken, the majority prevails. Usually the nine justices do not agree unanimously on a Court decision. Sometimes they vote 5 to 4 on a case, so the fate of an important issue may be decided by a single vote.

Justices who are on the winning side of a vote are called the majority; those on the losing side are the minority. If the chief justice has voted with the majority, he or she may write the *majority opinion,* which explains the Court decision. Or the chief justice may assign this task to another justice in the majority. If the chief justice has not voted with the majority, the senior justice voting with the majority will make the assignment. Justices who agree with the conclusion of the majority opinion but not with the reasons for reaching it may write *concurring opinions.* Any justice who disagrees with the majority decision may write a *dissenting opinion* to explain why he or she believes that the Court wrongly decided this case.

Often Supreme Court decisions are announced on Mondays during the last few weeks of the session. These decisions may have widespread effects that reach beyond the case that was considered. As soon as the High Court hands down a decision, all lower courts must follow this ruling in similar cases.

REVERSING THE COURT'S DECISIONS

The Supreme Court does not always rule the same way on the same or a closely related issue. The Court may rule one way at a certain time and later, in a similar case, render a much different decision.

The membership of the Court changes whenever a justice resigns or dies, and the justice appointed to fill this vacancy may have strikingly different views from those of the person being replaced. Also, changes and new developments are constantly occurring in our society, and they may bring with them new problems and concerns. As a result of these changes, justices may alter their attitudes and, from time to time, interpret the Constitution differently. "We are under a Constitution," declared Chief Justice Charles Evans Hughes, "but the Constitution is what the judges say it is."[1]

An important Supreme Court reversal pertained to the Court's interpretation of whether the Bill of Rights and the Fourteenth Amendment to the Constitution protect people from state, as well as national, violations of their rights. In a 1833 case, the Supreme Court ruled that the Bill of Rights could be applied only to strike down illegal actions taken by the national government.

More than thirty years later, the Fourteenth Amendment, ratified in 1868, laid the groundwork for eventually changing this interpretation and applying the Bill of Rights to safeguard citizens against state actions that infringed on their rights. One provision of this amendment says,". . . nor shall any State deprive any person of life, liberty, or property, without due process of law; nor deny to any person within its jurisdiction the equal protection of the laws." (The due process clause means, in general, that the government must act fairly and in accord with established, reasonable laws and legal procedures that do not violate the rights of citizens.)

In the latter part of the nineteenth century, the Supreme Court began interpreting the Fourteenth Amendment to protect private property rights against unfair state laws and regulations. But many more years passed before the Court started to apply the Bill of Rights and the Fourteenth Amendment's due process and equal protection clauses to other areas in which state governments curtailed the people's rights. Finally, in 1925, the Supreme Court decreed in the landmark case of *Gitlow* v. *New York* that freedom of speech and freedom of the press—which the First Amendment guards against violations by the national government—are also "among the fundamental personal rights and liberties protected by the due process clause of the Fourteenth Amendment from impairment by the States."

Since 1925, the Court has continued to adapt the Fourteenth Amendment to include other provisions of the Bill of Rights in curbing illegal state actions. One of the distinguishing trademarks of the nation's highest court in the past seventy years is the increased attention given to expanding the Bill of Rights to protect citizens against abuses caused by state governments.

TWO CONFLICTING VIEWPOINTS

Three chief justices have served on the Supreme Court in the past four decades—Earl Warren, Warren E. Burger, and William H. Rehnquist. The Warren Court extended from 1953 to 1969, the Burger Court from 1969 to 1986, and the Rehnquist Court from 1986 to the present. The Warren Court and the Rehnquist Court expressed conflicting viewpoints regarding how the High Court should exercise its power. The Warren Court was considered liberal and took an *activist* approach; the Rehnquist Court has generally been conservative and embraced a *traditionalist* philosophy. The Burger Court was in the middle—somewhat less activist than the Warren Court and somewhat less traditionalist than the Rehnquist Court.

Traditionalists favor judicial restraint and argue that the Supreme Court is, above all else, an institution dedicated to preserving continuity and stability. They put great faith in following *precedents,* believing that, as much as possible, the Court should refrain from reversing or modifying judicial decisions that have been made in the past. They tend to interpret the Constitution narrowly and try to base their judgments on what they believe the Founding Fathers intended when they wrote the supreme law of the land.

Defenders of judicial restraint would leave to Congress and the president—both elected by the people—the power to establish political, social, and economic policies. They maintain that the Supreme Court is neither a lawmaker nor a policy setter; its chief responsibility is to decide whether laws and lower court decisions are contrary to any provisions of the Constitution.

Judicial activists, on the other hand, believe that the Supreme Court should not be narrowly bound by traditions and precedents. They argue that the fact that the Court has already ruled on a specific issue is not always a sufficient reason why this issue cannot be raised again—and perhaps lead to a different decision.

Activists look at the Constitution broadly, contending that it is a living document that is flexible enough to meet the new challenges of our modern world. The Supreme Court, they assert, should play an important role in helping to bring about desirable political, social, and economic changes. For this reason, activists may expand the interpretation of stated rights to include other protections that are not specifically mentioned in the Constitution.

Justice William J. Brennan, Jr., who served thirty-four years on the Supreme Court, expressed the activists' interpretation of the Constitution when he said, "The ultimate question must be, what do the words mean in our time. For the genius of the Constitution rests not in any static meaning it might have had in a world that is dead and gone, but in the adaptability of its great principles to cope with current problems and current needs."[2]

Eight of the original members of the Warren Court had been nominated by Democratic presidents Franklin D. Roosevelt and Harry Truman; these activist justices handed down the most liberal decisions in the Court's history. But after Truman left office, only six Court appointments were made by other Democratic presidents between 1953 and 1994. For twenty-six of these years, Democratic chief executives did not have the opportunity to select a single justice. Meanwhile, Republican presidents between 1953 and 1993 appointed fifteen Court members.

After Republican Richard M. Nixon became president in 1969, he appointed four new justices, including Chief Justice Burger. The Court then began moving toward the center; it still embraced some parts of the Warren Court's activist philosophy, but it reversed or modified other parts. In 1981, Republican Ronald Reagan became president. He appointed three justices—all conservatives—and elevated conservative justice Rehnquist to serve as chief justice.

Following Reagan's administration, Republican president George Bush added one moderate, David H. Souter, and one conservative, Clarence Thomas, to the bench. By the time that Bush left office, in 1993, the conservative bloc constituted a clear majority of the justices.

President Bill Clinton, in the first two years of his administration, appointed Ruth Bader Ginsburg and Stephen G. Breyer to the Supreme Court. These new justices, who are generally considered quite liberal, replaced moderate conservative justice Byron R. White and liberal justice Harry A. Blackmun.

In some ways the conservative-dominated Rehnquist Court changed the direction of the Supreme Court. In other respects, however, the Rehnquist Court provided continuity by reinforcing earlier decisions made by the Warren Court and the Burger Court.

Now we will see how the Supreme Court has ruled during the past forty years in cases pertaining to eight subjects that are of great interest today: (1) freedom of religion, (2) the constitutionality of symbolic speech, (3) civil rights, (4) abortion, (5) sex discrimination, (6) the rights of the accused, (7) protection against illegal searches and seizures, and (8) capital punishment (the death penalty).

Attention is given to major rulings decreed by the Warren Court and the Burger Court. These earlier decisions provided important legacies that were handed down to the more recent Rehnquist Court.

CHAPTER TWO

FREEDOM OF RELIGION

The First Amendment to the United States Constitution includes two clauses concerning religion. One forbids laws respecting an establishment of religion. The other forbids laws prohibiting the free exercise of religion. These two brief clauses have been the source of some highly controversial Supreme Court decisions.

The establishment clause prevents the government from sponsoring any official religion and from promoting or aiding any religious groups. Thomas Jefferson firmly maintained that there must be a wall of separation between church and state in the United States, and at the time that the Constitution was being drafted James Madison declared that there was not to be "a shadow of right in the government to meddle with religion."[1] Cases pertaining to the establishment clause usually pose the question of whether the Supreme Court should strike down laws or government policies that are alleged to promote religion.

The free exercise clause protects the rights of Americans to worship (or not worship) as they please, without interference or restraints imposed by the government. At times, however, problems have arisen when certain religious beliefs and practices of individuals or minority groups have clashed with the standards followed by the majority of people. For example, in the nineteenth century, Mormons practiced polygamy while the rest of the population was governed by the law that restricted individuals to one spouse at a time. In this case, the Mormons were forced to give up polygamy and conform to the rule laid down by the majority. The free exercise clause has generally pertained to religious minorities and individuals who feel they are entitled to be exempted, or excused, from laws that interfere with their freedom to practice their religious beliefs.

THE ESTABLISHMENT OF RELIGION

LEGACY OF THE WARREN COURT

A landmark case concerning prayer in public schools was decided by the Warren Court in 1962. The school district of New Hyde Park, New York, had adopted a prayer to be recited daily in classrooms. This brief, nondenominational prayer consisted of the following words: "Almighty God, we acknowledge our dependence upon Thee, and we beg Thy blesssings upon us, our parents, our teachers, and our Country."

Even though recital of the prayer was voluntary, the parents of ten pupils in the district strongly objected to its use in public schools. They filed a lawsuit, contending that the prayer was contrary to their religious beliefs and practices and that it violated the establishment clause of the First Amendment.

When the case of *Engel* v. *Vitale* was considered by the Supreme Court, the justices voted 6 to 1 to declare the school prayer unconstitutional. Writing the opinion for the majority, Justice Hugo L. Black said that "the constitutional prohibition against laws respecting an establishment of religion must at least mean that in this country it is no part of the business of government to compose official prayers for any group of the American people to recite as a part of a religious program carried on by the government."

The Court's decision in *Engel* v. *Vitale* triggered a fierce protest from many Americans. Some demanded that the six justices in the majority resign or be impeached. Members of Congress introduced constitutional amendments to permit voluntary prayer in classrooms, but their amendments failed to secure enough votes for passage. The Roman Catholic prelate Francis Cardinal Spellman of New York declared that the prayer ruling "strikes at the very heart of the Godly tradition in which America's children have for so long been raised."[2] Evangelist Billy Graham asserted that "the framers of the Constitution meant we were to have freedom *of* religion, not freedom *from* religion."[3] Ironically, even though Justice Black was a devout Baptist and a Sunday-school teacher, he "was attacked in letters branding him 'Communistic,' 'Godless,' and 'atheistic.'"[4]

If prayers in public schools are unconstitutional, what about readings from the Bible? The Warren Court ruled on this question in 1963, the year after the *Engel* v. *Vitale* decision. A Pennsylvania law required classroom readings from the Bible each day, but pupils could be excused from this activity if their parents objected.

In the case of *School District of Abingdon Township* v. *Schempp,* the Supreme Court decreed, by a vote of 8 to 1, that the Bible readings were unconstitutional. The Court acknowledged that parts of the Bible could be taught as literature or history, but not as devotional exercises. Speaking for the Court majority, Justice Tom C. Clark wrote that these Bible readings were "in violation of the command of the First Amendment that the Government maintain strict neutrality, neither aiding nor opposing religion."

One of the most famous trials in American history occurred in 1925 when John Scopes was convicted for teaching Charles Darwin's theory of evolution to biology classes in violation of a Tennessee law that made it illegal to teach anything other than the literal biblical theory of human creation. While the state supreme court overturned Scopes's conviction, the issue of teaching evolution was not addressed by the U.S. Supreme Court until 1968, when it heard the case of *Epperson* v. *Arkansas.*

A biology teacher had contested an Arkansas law that prohibited teachers in public schools from discussing evolution or using textbooks that said anything about humankind ascending from a lower order of animals. The Court unanimously decreed that the Arkansas law violated the First Amendment.

LEGACY OF THE BURGER COURT

Another church-state matter that concerned the Supreme Court was whether state aid to parochial (religious) and other private schools was constitutional.

In *Lemon* v. *Kurtzman* (1971), the Court unanimously struck down two state laws—one in Rhode Island and one in Pennsylvania—permitting salary payments by the government to parochial school teachers and another state law providing reimbursement to parochial schools for teachers' salaries, textbooks, and instructional materials. As part of the Court opinion, Chief Justice Burger laid down a three-point test. He said that for government aid to be permissible to parochial schools, (1) it must have a secular (nonreligious) purpose; (2) its primary effect must neither promote nor undermine religion; and (3) it must not foster excessive government entanglement with religion.

Applying this three-point test, in 1973 the Supreme Court overturned New York laws that reimbursed poor parents of parochial school students for a portion of the school tuition and provided payments for maintenance and repairs to parochial schools. Twelve years later, the Burger Court ruled on two other cases that involved government assistance to nonpublic schools. It struck down a program in New York City that spent public funds to send teachers from public schools into parochial schools to enrich the teaching of secular subjects. The Court also decided that public school teachers in Grand Rapids, Michigan, could not be paid from tax money to hold classes for parochial and other private school students.

Another type of church-state case was decided in 1984. People in Pawtucket, Rhode Island, had displayed a Christian crèche, or Nativity scene, on government-owned property. The Burger Court had to determine whether the crèche violated the First Amendment or was a cultural symbol expressing peace and goodwill. By a 5 to 4 vote, the Court upheld the constitutionality of the Pawtucket Nativity scene. Justice Sandra Day O'Connor said that the Court majority believed it was important to differ-

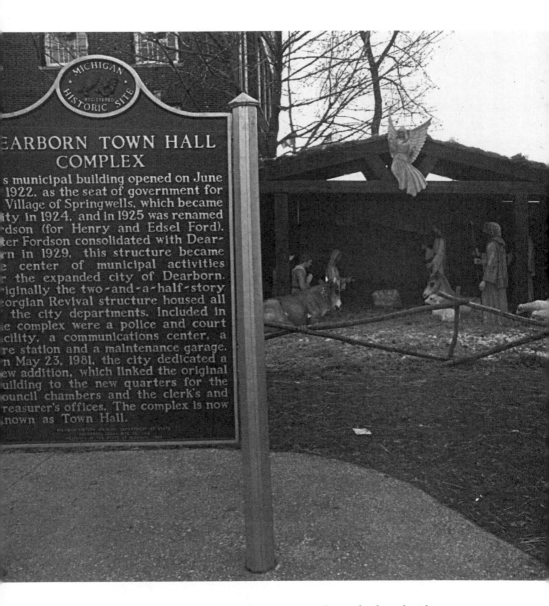

The sign reads:

MICHIGAN HISTORIC SITE
REGISTERED

EARBORN TOWN HALL
COMPLEX

s municipal building opened on June
1922, as the seat of government for
Village of Springwells, which became
ity in 1924, and in 1925 was renamed
·dson (for Henry and Edsel Ford).
ter Fordson consolidated with Dear-
rn in 1929, this structure became
e center of municipal activities
r the expanded city of Dearborn.
·iginally the two-and-a-half-story
·orgian Revival structure housed all
the city departments. Included in
e complex were a police and court
cility, a communications center, a
re station and a maintenance garage.
n May 23, 1981, the city dedicated a
ew addition, which linked the original
uilding to the new quarters for the
ouncil chambers and the clerk's and
reasurer's offices. The complex is now
nown as Town Hall.

In 1984 and again in 1989 the Supreme Court had to decide
whether religious Christmas scenes on public property violated the
First Amendment's separation of church and state. The Court did
not rule the same way in both cases.

entiate between government actions that accommodate, or make room for, religion and those that promote it.

The school prayer controversy surfaced again in 1985. The Alabama legislature had enacted a law that permitted a moment of silence for prayer or meditation at the beginning of each school day. People who favored prayer in public schools thought the Supreme Court probably would uphold this measure because it prescribed no specific words for the pupils to recite. But the justices voted 6 to 3 to overturn the Alabama law as a violation of the First Amendment prohibition against government establishment of religion. Writing for the majority in *Wallace* v. *Jaffree,* Justice John Paul Stevens said that it was established principle that the government must pursue a course of complete neutrality toward religion.

Justice Rehnquist opposed the majority opinion with a harsh dissent. He declared that Jefferson's claim that there must be a wall of separation between church and state "should be frankly and explicitly abandoned." Rehnquist asserted that the establishment clause of the First Amendment was intended only to prevent the creation of a national religion and to prohibit government preferences among religions. However, it does not "require government neutrality between religion and irreligion," Rehnquist wrote; nor does it prevent government "from providing nondiscriminatory aid to religion."

THE REHNQUIST COURT
Shortly after Rehnquist became chief justice, a religious issue was back before the Supreme Court, and again in a case from the Deep South. A Louisiana law ordered public school science teachers to give equal time—along with the teaching of the evolution theory—to teaching creation-science, the theory that God created humans in the manner described in the Bible. When high school science teacher Donald Aguillard, along with colleagues and some parents, contested the state law, both a federal district court and an appeals court declared it was unconstitutional. But Louisiana governor Edwin W. Edwards believed that the courts had been unfair to the supporters of creation-science. He maintained that his state's law, called the Balanced Treatment Act, did

nothing more than require the teaching of both theories of creation based on what he said was scientific, not religious, evidence. So Governor Edwards appealed the case to the Supreme Court.

The justices agreed, by a vote of 7 to 2, with the lower court decisions. Expressing the majority opinion in *Edwards* v. *Aguillard* (1987), Justice Brennan stated that it was clear that the purpose of the law was "to advance the religious viewpoint that a supernatural being created humankind." Consequently, the law's requirement that creation-science must be taught, Brennan wrote, "advances a religious doctrine" and "seeks to employ the symbolic and financial support of government to achieve a religious purpose."

The Court's two most conservative members, Chief Justice Rehnquist and Justice Antonin Scalia, dissented. Scalia sharply criticized his colleagues for declaring the law unconstitutional. "It was strongly supported by organized religions," he said. "Political activism by the religiously motivated is part of our heritage. Today's religious activism may give us [this law] . . . but yesterday's resulted in the abolition of slavery, and tomorrow's may bring relief for famine victims."

The Rehnquist Court in 1989 decided a case somewhat similar to the Pawtucket crèche case that the Burger Court had heard. In response to a suit filed by the American Civil Liberties Union (ACLU), a federal appeals court had decreed that public officials in Pittsburgh, Pennsylvania, may not display a crèche portraying Christ's birth and a Jewish menorah next to a Christmas tree at the city hall and county courthouse.

The Supreme Court was split into three groups on this case. Four conservatives—Chief Justice Rehnquist and Associate Justices White, Scalia, and Anthony M. Kennedy—approved the entire display and felt it did not defy the First Amendment. Three other justices—Brennan, Thurgood Marshall, and Stevens—would have struck down the whole display, including the Christmas tree, because it did not comply with the strict separation of church and state. Justices O'Connor and Blackmun pursued a middle course. O'Connor believed that only those decorations that appeared to endorse religion, such as the crèche, were unconstitutional. Blackmun saw nothing wrong with the

Christmas tree and said that since the menorah was displayed alongside the tree, "it would be a form of discrimination against Jews to allow Pittsburgh to celebrate Christmas as a cultural tradition while simultaneously disallowing the city's acknowledgement of Chanukah."

In *Allegheny County* v. *American Civil Liberties Union,* the justices handed down two rulings. They voted 5 to 4 that the crèche violated the First Amendment's establishment clause. But, on a 6 to 3 vote, they said it was not unconstitutional to display a menorah which appeared next to a secular Christmas tree. These confusing decisions caused one editorial writer to remark that "the state is taking an increasingly active role in erasing the religious Christmas and inflating the secular one starring Frosty, Santa, and Scrooge."[5]

The High Court decided another important religious case in 1992. A Rhode Island junior high school principal had invited a rabbi to deliver a brief invocation, or prayer, at graduation ceremonies. But a parent, Daniel Weisman, whose daughter Deborah was graduating, opposed the religious invocation at a public school commencement. He filed suit, and both a federal district court and a U.S. appeals court agreed with Weisman that the invocation violated the establishment clause of the First Amendment.

When the case reached the Supreme Court, many constitutional experts predicted that the justices would uphold the invocation. By this time, the Rehnquist Court included seven members who were generally regarded as conservatives. President Bush and leaders of the Justice Department thought that the conservative justices would seize this opportunity to reverse the thirty-year-old Warren Court ban on prayer in public schools. Supporters of school prayer especially counted on the vote of Justice Kennedy, who had dissented in the Pittsbugh crèche case, arguing that the Court should permit such displays and follow "policies of accommodation, acknowledgment, and support for religion."

Justice Kennedy, however, and Justices O'Connor and Souter deserted the conservative bloc on this issue and opposed the school invocation. By a 5 to 4 margin in *Lee* v. *Weisman,* the

Supreme Court decided that the prayer was contrary to the First Amendment. Justice Kennedy wrote the majority opinion in which he said that "the Constitution guarantees that government may not coerce anyone to support or participate in religion or its exercise." A school-sponsored invocation, Kennedy contended, "may appear to the nonbeliever or dissenter to be an attempt . . . to enforce a religious orthodoxy."

In a scathing dissent, Justice Scalia declared that the Court's decision treats religion "as some purely personal avocation that can be indulged entirely in secret, like pornography, in the privacy of one's room." He argued that a ceremonial prayer can unify the community and "inoculate [it] from religious bigotry and prejudice."

Another school prayer case was appealed to the Supreme Court in 1993. In this case, the students at a high school in Houston, Texas, had voted to permit a member of the senior class to deliver a nonsectarian prayer at the graduation ceremonies. The chief difference between this case and the 1992 prayer case was that the Houston students had acted on their own to include a prayer at graduation, but in the earlier case school officials had sponsored a prayer delivered by a clergyman. A federal appeals court in Texas ruled that the student-initiated prayer at the Houston high school had not violated the First Amendment. The Supreme Court refused to consider this case, which meant that it accepted the ruling of the appeals court that the prayer was not prohibited by the Constitution.

In 1993, the Rehnquist Court decided a case involving the use of school facilities by a religious group. A New York State school district had a policy that permitted community civic groups to use its auditorium for evening programs but denied the same privilege to religious groups on the grounds that this would violate the separation of church and state. A Christian group sued the school district when it denied use of the auditorium for a program featuring church speakers and the showing of a religious film. Both a federal district court and a U.S. appeals court had upheld the school district's policy. The Supreme Court, however, struck down the policy that permitted the use of school facilities in the evening for nonreligious functions but banned a similar use by religious groups. This decision was reached by a unanimous vote of the justices.

Speaking for the Court, Justice White wrote, "The government violates the First Amendment when it denies access to a speaker solely to suppress the point of view he expresses." Permitting a religious group to meet at a school, White asserted, is not a situation in which the school district can be accused of "endorsing religion or any particular creed."

The Rehnquist Court was closely divided on a 1993 case pertaining to the use of tax money to pay for a deaf student's sign-language interpreter in a school operated by a religious group. In Tucson, Arizona, parents of the deaf son had enrolled him in a Catholic school because they wanted him to have religious instruction. They paid the cost for the interpreter but then sued the school district when they were not reimbursed for this cost. Both a federal judge and the Ninth Circuit Court of Appeals ruled that using public funds to pay for an interpreter in a private parochial school violated the constitutional separation of church and state. But by a vote of 5 to 4, the Supreme Court reversed the decision of the lower courts in *Zobrest* v. *Catalina Foothills School District* and ordered that the school district must pay the cost of the interpreter.

Writing the majority opinion, Chief Justice Rehnquist declared that the Constitution "lays down no absolute bar to the placing of a public employee in a private school." He asserted that a "neutral government program" that reimburses parents does not violate the Constitution simply because the payment of such funds may benefit a parochial school.

In a joint dissent, Justices Blackmun and Souter expressed concern that the Court for the first time had authorized a public employee to "participate directly in religious indoctrination."

A major church-state case was decided in 1994, when the Supreme Court considered whether the creation of a small school district to accommodate the needs of a religious sect violated the establishment clause of the First Amendment. A group of Orthodox Jews known as the Satmar Hasidic sect began settling in the mid-1970s in a rustic community about fifty miles north of New York City. Most of their children went to parochial schools, but the Hasidic Jews believed that their children who had disabilities needed special facilities that were equipped to cope with the children's handicaps. So in 1989 the state of New York established the tiny, one-building Kiryas Joel Village School District for these disabled students.

This school district's expenses, like those of other school districts, were paid for with public funds. In 1990, Louis Grumet, executive director of the New York State School Boards Association, sued the Kiryas Joel Village School District, saying public money should not be used to support religion. The New York state courts agreed with Grumet that this special school district for a religious sect violated the separation of church and state.

By a vote of 6 to 3, the Supreme Court ruled that the law setting up this school district amounted to illegal favoritism toward religion in general and toward one sect in particular. Expressing the majority opinion, Justice Souter said that this special school district for Hasidic Jews violated "a principle at the heart of the Establishment Clause, that government should not prefer one religion to another or religion to irreligion." He explained that establishing a school district for one religious sect was a special favor that other religious groups or other villages organized on nonreligious lines would not receive.

The three dissenters were Chief Justice Rehnquist and Justices Scalia and Clarence Thomas. Justice Scalia wrote, "The history of the populating of North America is in no small measure the story of groups of people sharing a common religious and cultural heritage striking out to form their own communities. It is preposterous to suggest that the civil institutions of these communities, separate from their churches, were constitutionally suspect [regarded with suspicion]."

While some other rulings of the Rehnquist Court suggested that the government could allow certain religious practices in public institutions, such as student-initiated prayers at graduation ceremonies, in *Board of Education* v. *Grumet* it struck down a law that gave preference to a particular religious sect.

THE FREE EXERCISE OF RELIGION

LEGACY OF THE WARREN COURT

One matter that came before the Warren Court was determining which religious beliefs qualified a man to be exempted from mandatory military service (the draft). The conscription laws passed by Congress in World Wars I and II exempted conscientious objectors whose opposition to war was based on religious training and beliefs. In 1948, Congress clarified the draft law by adding a provision that said grounds for exemption were to be based on beliefs that involved "a relation to a Supreme Being."

When Donald Seeger asked to be classified as a conscientious objector in 1957, he said he was opposed to participation in any war because of his religious beliefs. But Seeger declared that his "religious" opposition to war was based on his reading books by philosophers rather than a belief in God, and he asserted that religious convictions could be strongly held without belonging to any particular church. Since Seeger acknowledged no "relation to a Supreme Being," his draft board refused to classify him as a conscientious objector. When he refused to report for military service, Seeger was tried in court and found guilty of violating the draft law. A U.S. court of appeals reversed his conviction, but the federal government then appealed the case to the Supreme Court.

Eight years after Seeger first sought exemption from military service, the Court overturned his conviction. Justice Clark wrote the majority opinion in *United States* v. *Seeger* (1965). He said that the "test of belief 'in a relation to a Supreme Being' is whether a given belief that is sincere and meaningful occupies a place in the life of its possessor parallel to that filled by the orthodox belief in God of one who clearly qualifies for exemption."

LEGACY OF THE BURGER COURT

In 1970, during the Vietnam War, the Burger Court expanded the draft exemption to include persons who objected to all war on moral and ethical grounds. The following year, however, it ruled that a man could be drafted if his only opposition to military service stemmed from the belief that a particular war was unjust. The Court ruled that the damage of infringing on religious freedom when a person claimed that a particular war was unjust was outweighed by the government's need to maintain an efficient, fairly administered draft operation.

The Court was confronted in 1972 by a case concerning the Amish religious sect. The Amish parents in Wisconsin refused to send their children to public school beyond the eighth grade. They claimed that high school education fostered the teaching of secular ideas harmful to their spiritual beliefs and belittled their tradition of living in tightly organized religious communities set apart from worldly influences. The state of Wisconsin contended that the Amish were breaking the compulsory school attendance law, and the trial court supported the state's argument.

The Supreme Court, however, overturned this verdict, maintaining that traditional Amish beliefs could suffer by compelling students of this sect to attend high school. Writing the majority opinion in *Wisconsin* v. *Yoder,* Chief Justice Burger said that a ". . . state's interest in universal education, however highly we rank it, is not totally free from a balancing process when it impinges on fundamental rights and interests, such as those specifically protected by the Free Exercise Clause of the First Amendment, and the traditional interest of parents with respect to the religious upbringing of their children."

A different type of religious case came before the Burger Court in 1986. Former Air Force captain S. Simcha Goldman had often worn a yarmulke (a Jewish scullcap) while serving as a rabbi at a military hospital. Although Air Force regulations generally forbade the wearing of nonmilitary attire while in uniform, Goldman refused to stop wearing the yarmulke on duty. He declared that this practice was a religious observance common among Orthodox and Conservative Jews. The rabbi was then threatened with court-martial and left the service. He brought suit against the government, claiming that the First Amendment protected his right to wear religious apparel unless it presented a clear danger to discipline. Government attorneys disputed this claim, contending that permission to wear yarmulkes would detract from the uniformity required by dress regulations.

By a narrow margin of 5 to 4, the Supreme Court upheld the Air Force regulation in *Goldman* v. *Weinberger, Secretary of*

Defense. Justice Rehnquist, writing for the majority, said that Air Force rules reasonably and evenhandedly regulate dress in the interest of the military's perceived need for uniformity and that the application of the rules to Goldman did not violate the First Amendment, even though it did restrict the exercise of his religious beliefs. Justice Brennan, one of the dissenters, asserted that it surpasses belief that yarmulkes would undermine military discipline.

THE REHNQUIST COURT

Until 1990, the Supreme Court used a balancing test to determine whether persons should be exempt from laws that interfered with their religious beliefs. If they could show that a law seriously hindered a major aspect of their religion, they would be exempt unless the state proved that the law served a "compelling government interest." Thus, the Court had exempted the Amish from Wisconsin's compulsory school attendance law after the eighth grade when it was shown that this law would gravely endanger their religious beliefs and there was no compelling government interest in forcing the Amish teenagers to attend high school.

This balancing test was reviewed again by the Court in a 1990 case. Alfred Smith, a Native American, and his friend, Galen Black, a non-Native American who had become a member of a Native American church, both admitted they had ingested peyote as part of a customary ceremony prescribed by their religion. Peyote is a stimulant drug; it produces hallucinations, much as LSD does.

Because they had used peyote, both men lost their jobs as drug counselors, and the state of Oregon refused to give them unemployment benefits since they had been dismissed for alleged misconduct. They sued on the grounds that their free exercise of religion had been violated, and the supreme court of Oregon upheld their claim.

When their case was appealed to the U.S. Supreme Court, the justices voted 5 to 4 to overturn the Oregon court's decision. Furthermore, the Rehnquist Court rejected the long-established balancing test and declared that laws that strike down a religious practice need not be justified by a compelling government interest.

Expressing the majority opinion in *Oregon v. Smith and Black,* Justice Scalia said, "Any society . . . would be courting anarchy" if it tried to shield all religious practices and decided to "coerce or suppress none of them." Scalia wanted state governments to decide which religious practices, such as the use of peyote, should be exempted from their laws. He conceded that leaving these decisions to state governments could put religious minorities at a disadvantage. Nevertheless, he asserted that the "unavoidable consequence of democratic government must be preferred to a system in which each conscience is a law unto itself or in which judges weigh the social importance of all laws against . . . all religious beliefs."

In a sharply worded dissent, Justice O'Connor wrote that the majority decision, which "dramatically departs from well-settled First Amendment [rulings], appears unnecessary to resolve the question presented," and is not consistent "with our Nation's fundamental commitment to individual religious liberty." Her dissent was joined by Justices Brennan, Marshall, and Blackmun.

The Rehnquist Court in 1993 rendered another major decision on a case involving the "free exercise of religion." The followers of Santeria, an Afro-Cuban religion, practice the ceremonial killing of goats, chickens, sheep, ducks and other animals as part of their religious rituals. About fifty thousand Santerians have settled in south Florida, and some of their neighbors objected to the slaughtering of animals in a religious ceremony. In 1987, the city of Hialeah, Florida, adopted a ban on animal sacrifice as a result of a public outcry over the plan of some Santerians to put up a building on a downtown lot as a place to conduct sacrifices.

The church's leaders filed a lawsuit claiming that Hialeah's ordinance (law) infringed on the Santerians' religious rights guaranteed by the First Amendment. They also argued that it was inconsistent to prevent them from killing animals while permitting such means of ending animals' lives as hunting, commercial slaughter, pest control, and putting to death stray or sick dogs and cats. The city officials responded that the Santerians kept their animals in filthy pens, killed them cruelly by severing their neck arteries, and failed to dispose of the carcasses in a sanitary manner. Both a federal district court and an appeals court upheld the Hialeah ordinance.

When the case reached the Supreme Court, Douglas Laycock, the lawyer for the Santerians, told the justices, "This is a case about open discrimination against a minority religion." He declared that the ban on animal sacrifice was adopted for "the express purpose of preventing the central ritual of this faith."[6] The justices agreed with this point of view and voted unanimously that the Hialeah ordinance was unconstitutional.

CHAPTER THREE

SYMBOLIC SPEECH

Freedom of speech, guaranteed by the First Amendment, has been upheld in Supreme Court decisions for many years. In more recent times, the Court has frequently considered whether nonoral expression, known as symbolic speech, is also safeguarded by the First Amendment and by the Fourteenth Amendment's due process clause.

Symbolic speech includes such matters as wearing armbands as an expression of protest, burning or in some other way defiling the American flag, taking part in mass demonstrations to oppose some law or government policy, and burning crosses on the lawns of blacks as a sign of racial bigotry. To what extent should these nonspoken expressions—even those that are offensive to a large segment of the American public—be protected? The court system and ultimately the Supreme Court have had to answer this question.

LEGACY OF THE WARREN COURT

Southern segregationists tried to use state laws and local ordinances against disturbance of the peace as barriers to the protests that were mounted as part of the civil rights movement of the 1960s. But their actions often were overturned by the Supreme

Court. Sit-in demonstrations at "whites only" lunch counters were declared constitutional by a unanimous decision of the Warren Court in *Garner* v. *Louisiana* (1961). Speaking for the Court, Justice John Marshall Harlan stated that a sit-in was "as much a part of the 'free trade in ideas' . . . as is verbal expression, more commonly thought of as 'speech.'" Justice Harlan emphasized the legitimate nature of symbolic speech, saying that "this Court has never limited the right to speak . . . to mere verbal expression."

In *Edwards* v. *South Carolina* (1963), the Court decided a case involving the arrest of students who had held a mass demonstration on the public grounds of the statehouse. Disregarding a police order to leave, they remained on the grounds, singing patriotic and religious songs and listening to talks. The South Carolina law that they had allegedly defied forbade demonstrations and symbolic speech that "stirred people to anger, invited public dispute, or brought about a condition of unrest."

With only one dissent, the Supreme Court ruled in favor of the demonstrators. Justice Potter Stewart, generally considered one of the more conservative members of the Warren Court, wrote the majority opinion. He stated that the South Carolina law violated the "constitutionally protected rights of free speech, free assembly, and freedom to petition for redress [removing the cause] of their grievances."

Opposition to the Vietnam War generated important symbolic speech cases. One case, *United States* v. *O'Brien* (1968), concerned a young man who had burned his draft card to protest the war and the draft. He asserted that this action was an expression of symbolic speech protected by the First Amendment. The Supreme Court, however, upheld the man's conviction. It declared that "when 'speech and nonspeech' elements are combined in the same course of conduct, a sufficiently important governmental interest in regulating the nonspeech element can justify incidental limitations on First Amendment freedoms." Thus, the Court affirmed that the government had a sufficiently important interest in maintaining the draft registration system to warrant the need for criminally prosecuting violators who destroyed draft cards.

In the 1960s, some opponents of the war in Vietnam
burned their draft cards, asserting that this was an expression of
symbolic speech protected by the First Amendment. In
United States v. *O'Brien* (1968) the Supreme Court upheld the
conviction of a draft card burner.

Another case pertaining to the Vietnam War arose after some students in Des Moines, Iowa, wore black armbands to school as a symbolic protest against the war. The principals of the Des Moines schools, fearing that the armbands might trigger student disturbances and demonstrations, agreed on a regulation to suspend pupils wearing armbands. But thirteen-year-old Mary Beth Tinker and a few other youths defied this regulation and continued wearing armbands, which resulted in their suspension from school. The students, through their parents, contested in a lawsuit that their First Amendment rights had been violated.

When the case was appealed to the Supreme Court in 1969, the justices, by a vote of 7 to 2, upheld the constitutional rights of the students to wear armbands. Justice Abe Fortas, writing the majority opinion in *Tinker* v. *Des Moines Independent Community School District,* asserted that neither students nor teachers "shed their constitutional rights to freedom of speech or expression at the schoolhouse gate." The Court held that student expression could be punished only if it would materially and substantially interfere with schoolwork or with the rights of others.

In *Street* v. *New York* (1969), the Warren Court heard the first case in modern times regarding abuse of the American flag. It involved a black man in Brooklyn, New York, who, after hearing about the shooting of civil rights leader James Meredith, rushed into a street and burned a flag. "If they did that to Meredith," he angrily declared, "we don't need an American flag." Street was found guilty under a New York State law making it illegal to mutilate a flag or cast contempt upon it either by words or conduct.

By a 5 to 4 vote, the Supreme Court reversed Street's conviction. It said that the New York law as applied to Street was too broad because it permitted the punishment of a person's words, which were protected by the First and Fourteenth Amendments. The Warren Court, however, sidestepped the issue of whether burning the flag could also be constitutionally protected. Ironically, three of the most liberal Court members—Chief Justice Warren and Associate Justices Black and Fortas—were among the dissenters in this case. Warren wrote in dissent, "I believe that the States and the Federal Government do have the power to protect the flag from acts of desecration and disgrace."

LEGACY OF THE BURGER COURT

Two other flag cases were heard by the Burger Court in the 1970s. One case involved a Massachusetts man who wore a small flag on the seat of his pants. The other case pertained to a Washington student who flew a flag, on which he had placed a peace symbol, upside down from his apartment window. Both Massachusetts and Washington had laws forbidding defacement of the flag, and the men were convicted for breaking these laws.

The Supreme Court overturned both convictions as violations of the First Amendment. The Court held that although these unorthodox displays might be offensive to some persons who saw them, they did not clash with any government interest that warranted restraint of symbolic speech.

While the Burger Court's decisions on the flag issues represented a liberal point of view, the Court took a conservative stance in the 1986 case of a high school senior, Matthew Fraser, who was suspended for giving an allegedly lewd speech at a school assembly. Fraser said no obscene words, but he did make some sexual allusions in his talk. He fought his school suspension in the courts, claiming that his conduct caused no substantial disruption and therefore was protected by the precedent that the Court had set in the previous *Tinker* case. Both a federal district court and an appeals court ruled in favor of Fraser.

A majority of the justices on the Supreme Court disagreed. By a 7 to 2 vote, they upheld the school's disciplinary action against the student. The Burger Court distinguished between the "sexual content" of Fraser's speech and the "political message" of the students who wore armbands to protest the Vietnam War in the *Tinker* case. Expressing the opinion of the majority, Chief Justice Burger declared that school authorities can "prohibit the use of vulgar and offensive terms" and determine what manner of speech in the school assembly "is appropriate."

In a dissenting opinion, Justice Stevens suggested that the Court majority had applied moral standards to this case that might have been appropriate at an earlier time but could be considered too prudish and restrictive in the 1980s. Stevens reminded his colleagues that when the movie *Gone With the Wind* was first shown in the 1930s, the expression "Frankly, I don't give a damn" was considered immoral and shocking by many people.

THE REHNQUIST COURT

One of the first symbolic speech cases heard by the Rehnquist Court pertained to the solicitation of pamphlets. Avi Snyder, a minister for Jews for Jesus, had been forbidden to pass out religious leaflets in the terminal of the Los Angeles airport. Because of the large crowds at the busy terminal and the chance that solicitors could block corridors or disturb passengers, the board of airport commissioners had adopted a policy in 1983 that the terminal area "is not open for First Amendment activities by any individual or entity."

Snyder filed a lawsuit to determine whether his constitutional rights had been denied. When the case was appealed to the Supreme Court in 1987, the justices unanimously decreed that the airport regulation was unconstitutional. Speaking for the Court, Justice O'Connor said that the ban on all "First Amendment activities" in the airport terminal could "prohibit even talking and reading or the wearing of campaign buttons or symbolic clothing. . . . No conceivable government interest, O'Connor declared, would justify such an absolute prohibition of speech."

In 1989, the Rehnquist Court was confronted by a very important flag-burning case, and this time the central issue was not sidestepped, as the Warren Court had done twenty years earlier in the *Street* decision. The case involved Gregory ("Joey") Johnson, a member of the Revolutionary Communist Youth Brigade, who had torched an American flag outside the 1984 Republican convention arena in Dallas, Texas. As the flag

Although many Americans are appalled by the burning of the flag, the Supreme Court ruled in 1989 that it is a form of free expression protected by the First Amendment.

burned to ashes, other protesters shouted, "America, the red, white, and blue, we spit on you." Johnson was convicted of breaking a Texas law that forbade the deliberate destruction of the flag, and this law stipulated that violators would be subject to a punishment of up to one year in jail and a $2,000 fine. At that time, forty-eight states and the federal government had laws that prohibited the intentional defacement or mutilation of the national flag.

The Supreme Court, by a close 5 to 4 vote, overturned Johnson's conviction. Surprisingly, two conservative justices appointed by President Reagan—Scalia and Kennedy—joined liberals Brennan, Marshall, and Blackmun to form the majority. Chief Justice Rehquist dissented, along with O'Connor, Stevens, and White. The Court's decision was based on the premise that burning the flag was a permissible form of symbolic speech, even if it incurred the wrath of many Americans.

"If there is a bedrock principle underlying the First Amendment," wrote Brennan for the majority, "it is that Government may not prohibit the expression of an idea offensive or disagreeable." In a separate opinion, Kennedy said, "It is poignant but fundamental that the flag protects those who hold it in contempt."

Dissenter Rehnquist rejected the premise that flag burning was a constitutionally protected form of symbolic speech and angrily called it the "equivalent of an inarticulate grunt or roar." In a separate dissent, Stevens asserted that the flag as a symbol was "worthy of protection from unnecessary desecration."

The decision in *Texas* v. *Johnson* unleashed a torrent of enraged criticism. "Flag burning is wrong—dead wrong," declared President Bush.[1] "Nobody, but nobody, should ever deface the American flag," shouted an American Legion member who had fought in World War II and Korea.[2] A *Newsweek* poll showed that 71 percent of the people would support a constitutional amendment making flag burning illegal.[3] Senate Republican leader Bob Dole asserted, "People are saying keep your hands off Old Glory."[4] By a vote of 97 to 3, the Senate passed a resolution expressing profound disappointment with the ruling.[5]

Not all Americans, however, condemned the Court's stand on flag burning. "James Madison, who wrote the First Amendment, would have his heart warmed by the decision," said David O'Brien, a political science professor at the University of Virginia, "but he would have been appalled that it was a 5 to 4 vote."[6] David Cole, one of the lawyers who defended the flag burner, declared, "If free expression is to exist in this county, people must be as free to burn the flag as they are to wave it."[7]

Congress responded quickly by passing the Flag Protection Act, making it a crime to knowingly mutilate, deface, or burn the flag. When the law was violated, the Supreme Court once again was called upon to deal with the flag burning issue. In *U.S. v. Eichman* (1990), the justices, by the same 5 to 4 vote, ruled this new law was unconstitutional. This time, the public outcry was muted because it had become obvious that flag burning could be ended only by a constitutional amendment, which requires the lengthy, difficult process of obtaining a two-thirds vote of both houses of Congress followed by ratification by three fourths of the states.

On a night in October 1990, a teenager, Robert A. Viktora, and several friends burned a wooden cross on the lawn of a black family that had recently moved to a mostly white working-class neighborhood in St. Paul, Minnesota. Viktora was arrested for violating a St. Paul ordinance (law) that forbade placing on public or private property any symbol that could arouse anger, alarm, or resentment in others on the basis of race, color, creed, religion, or gender. Before Viktora could be tried in court, his attorneys challenged the ordinance as unconstitutional. The trial court and the Minnesota Supreme Court upheld the ordinance, but the teenager's attorneys then appealed to the nation's highest court.

When the Rehnquist Court decided *R.A.V. v. St. Paul* in 1992, all nine justices voted to overturn the St. Paul ordinance. The Court decreed that the government cannot punish those who communicate messages of racial, gender, or religious intolerance simply because such ideas are offensive to most Americans. The justices agreed that Viktora's hate crime was despicable and deserved punishment, but they argued that he should have been charged with arson, trespass, or damage to property—not with expressing an unpopular opinion. The First Amendment forbids "silencing speech on the basis of its content," wrote Justice Scalia.

"The government," he said, may not regulate the use of speech "based on hostility—or favoritism—towards the underlying message expressed."

The Supreme Court ruling in this "hate-crime" case appeared to strike down laws in many states that made it a crime to burn a cross, exhibit a Nazi swastika, or display messages on signs or T-shirts that express bigotry. But the Court left unresolved whether state judges could impose longer jail terms on those whose violent crimes, such as assault, are motivated by a bias against blacks, Jews, homosexuals, or other minorities.

In 1993, however, the Supreme Court finally agreed to rule on whether judges could impose longer prison sentences on defendants whose physical attacks on innocent persons were motivated by their victims' race, religion, national origin, gender, or sexual orientation. Twenty-six states had laws permitting stiffer punishment for assaults based on bigotry. But the constitutionality of these laws had been in doubt because of the possibility that the Supreme Court might decree that increasing the sentence for a violent hate crime infringed on the defendant's right of free expression.

The hate-crime case that the Rehnquist Court reviewed stemmed from a brutal incident in 1989 after a group of young black men in Kenosha, Wisconsin, left a theater in which they had seen *Mississippi Burning,* a film about the persecution of blacks in the 1960s. One of the men, Todd Mitchell, allegedly said to his friends, "Do you all feel hyped up to move on some white people?" Spotting a fourteen-year-old white youth across the street, he announced, "There goes a white boy. Go get him!" Then Mitchell led his friends in attacking the youth and beating him so badly that he suffered brain damage.

Mitchell was tried and convicted of aggravated assault. After sentencing him to two years in prison for the beating, the judge also punished him for his motive. Applying a Wisconsin law that permits increased penalties for hate crimes, the judge extended Mitchell's prison sentence to four years. But the Wisconsin Supreme Court rejected the extra two-year sentence, ruling that the state's hate-crime law violated the First Amendment's freedom of speech clause because it imposed additional punishment for Mitchell's statements.

Some legal experts disagreed with this court decision and considered Wisconsin's hate-crime law reasonable and necessary. "The absolute right to think and believe what you want," said Harvard law professor Laurence Tribe, "and to express any viewpoint, however hateful, has nothing to do with some kind of license [permission] to target victims of violence based on their race, sex, religion, or sexual orientation."[8]

In a unanimous decision, the U.S. Supreme Court ruled that Wisconsin's hate-crime law was constitutional. Speaking for the Court, Chief Justice Rehnquist drew a clear distinction between acceptable and unacceptable symbolic speech. He explained that laws which make it a crime to burn a cross or an American flag are "explicitly directed at expression," and the Supreme Court has found such laws unconstitutional. On the other hand, laws imposing a longer sentence for bigotry-motivated assault are "aimed at conduct" and are constitutional. "A physical assault," declared the chief justice, "is not by any stretch of the imagination expressive conduct protected by the First Amendment."

The Supreme Court in 1994 decided a symbolic speech case pertaining to displaying political messages on signs. The city of Ladue, Missouri, a wealthy suburb of St. Louis, had enacted a ban on nearly all signs and billboards in order to combat "visual blight" and protect the heavily wooded, rustic appearance of the community. The only exceptions to the Ladue ordinance were road signs, identifications for buildings such as hospitals, schools, and churches, and "for sale" or "for rent" signs in front of homes. In 1990, Margaret Gilleo, a Ladue resident, put on her front lawn a sign that read: "Say No to War in the Persian Gulf. Call Congress Now." She put a similar sign in her house's second-story window.

Some neighbors objected to the signs and when city officials told her they were illegal, Gilleo filed a lawsuit claiming that her First Amendment rights had been violated. A federal judge then struck down the Ladue ordinance as unconstitutional, and a U.S. appeals court upheld this ruling.

The Supreme Court voted unanimously that Gilleo had the right to express her political beliefs on signs posted on her property. Speaking for the Court, Justice Stevens observed that lawn signs "are an unusually cheap and convenient form of communication" the First Amendment was meant to protect.

CHAPTER FOUR

CIVIL RIGHTS

The Thirteenth Amendment (1865) ended slavery, the Fourteenth Amendment (1868) promised the equal protection of the laws for all Americans, and the Fifteenth Amendment (1870) said that the right of citizens to vote shall not be denied on account of race or color. Yet for many years after these amendments were adopted, blacks in the South (and to a lesser degree in other parts of the country) were treated as separate, second-class citizens. African Americans throughout the South were forbidden to attend the schools and colleges that educated white students. Blacks were segregated in restaurants, hotels, theaters, and ballparks, on streetcars, buses, and trains, in municipal parks and swimming pools, and even in the use of depot waiting rooms, toilets, and water fountains. Despite the Fifteenth Amendment, blacks in southern states were denied the vote by such devices as the poll tax, property and literacy tests, and the so-called "grandfather clause" that restricted the ballot to only those persons whose grandfathers had been eligible to vote.

Blatant segregation actually was upheld by the Supreme Court in a major 1898 decision. The Court decreed in *Plessy* v. *Ferguson,* with only one dissenting vote, that the Fourteenth Amendment "could not have been intended to abolish distinc-

tions based upon color, or to enforce social . . . equality. . . . Laws permitting, and even requiring [the separation of races] in places where they are liable to be brought into contact do not necessarily imply the inferiority of either race to the other, and have been generally recognized as within the competency of the state legislatures in the exercise of their police powers." The Supreme Court in this decision approved a "separate but equal" doctrine intended to justify state-imposed racial segregation. It maintained that if the facilities provided blacks were equal to those provided whites, segregation by state or local laws did not violate the Constitution.

For more than half a century this separate but equal doctrine prevailed and effectively restrained efforts to advance civil rights in the nation's courts. It was not reversed until the Warren Court decided the landmark case *Brown* v. *Board of Education of Topeka* in 1954.

LEGACY OF THE WARREN COURT

Linda Brown, a young black girl in Topeka, Kansas, had to walk twenty blocks to an all-black elementary school rather than attend an all-white public school much nearer to her home. This was because, under Kansas law, cities with more than fifteen thousand residents were permitted to operate segregated school systems, providing the schools were substantially equal in educational facilities. Topeka was one of the cities that had separate primary schools for blacks and whites.

In 1951, Oliver Brown, Linda's father, sued Topeka's board of education on the grounds that its segregated schools violated his daughter's constitutional right to the equal protection of the laws. A federal district court declared that Topeka's practice of segrega-

Linda Brown, whose father sued Topeka's board of education on grounds that its policy of school segregation violated his daughter's constitutional rights

tion was detrimental to black children. However, the district court could find no constitutional violation because the schools for blacks and whites were substantially equal with respect to buildings, equipment, teachers, and subjects taught.

When *Brown* v. *Board of Education* reached the Supreme Court, it was lumped with four other segregation cases of a similar nature from Virginia, South Carolina, Delaware, and the District of Columbia. So whatever ruling the Court handed down would apply not just to Topeka, but to the whole nation. Two of the country's ablest attorneys argued *Brown* and its companion cases before the Warren Court. The chief attorney representing the segregationists was John W. Davis, a distinguished lawyer who had served as a congressman from West Virginia, a U.S. solicitor general, an ambassador to Great Britain, and the Democratic nominee for the presidency in 1924. His opponent before the High Court was the brilliant Thurgood Marshall, the country's foremost African-American attorney and director of the Legal Defense and Educational Fund of the National Association for the Advancement of Colored People (NAACP). (In 1967, Marshall became the first black member of the Supreme Court.)

In perhaps the most significant, far-reaching decision in the history of the Supreme Court, the justices decided unanimously in 1954 that segregation by race in public schools is unconstitutional. Speaking for the Court, Chief Justice Warren declared, ". . . We conclude that in the field of public education the doctrine of 'separate but equal' has no place. Separate educational facilities are inherently unequal." In this one momentous decision, the Court had ruled not only in favor of Linda Brown and the other African-American students in similar cases, but it had also opened the door to the promotion of civil rights in many other areas of American society.

The *Brown* decision was highly praised by African Americans and many other people outside the South. Teacher and author G. Theodore Mitau expressed the opinion that it "acknowledged judicially what many people had known or felt for a long time: segregation was morally indefensible, socially irrational and politically undemocratic. It perpetuated a racial myth which impris-

The Warren Court's ruling on the unconstitutionality of
segregated public schools was perhaps the most significant,
far-reaching decision in the history of the Supreme Court.

oned American values at home and weakened America's leadership abroad."[1]

Whites in the South, however, were stunned by the *Brown*
ruling. Historian C. Vann Woodward exclaimed that "something
very much like panic seized many parts of the South . . . a panic
bred of insecurity and fear."[2] Southern politicians urged their
constituents to defy the Court and call for the impeachment of
Chief Justice Warren. A document commonly known as the
"Southern Manifesto" was signed by 101 of 128 members of

Congress from eleven southern and border states. It attempted to unite the South behind the belief that *Brown* was a clear abuse of judicial power and said, in effect, that southerners "are not going to obey this edict from the Supreme Court and will do everything in [their] power to wipe it out."[3]

While *Brown* called for drastic changes in the enrollment policies of southern schools, it did not explain when or how these changes were to take place. So, the following year, the Warren Court invited the chief lawyers in the *Brown* case to reappear and argue the question of implementing the landmark decision. After the justices had listened to the arguments, they handed down their 1955 ruling in what has been called *Brown* II. Again voting unanimously and again speaking through the chief justice, the Court set no specific date for the integration of public schools. Desegregation, the chief justice explained, had to await solutions of such problems as providing the transportation of pupils, constructing buildings large enough to accommodate both black and white students, and redrawing boundaries for school districts. Nevertheless, the Court ruled that states should proceed to end segregation with "all deliberate speed." Ordering integration with "all deliberate speed" was such a vague statement that most southern states moved very slowly in implementing desegregation. As late as 1964, a decade after *Brown* I, only 2.3 percent of southern black children attended desegregated schools.[4]

In *Brown* II, the Court placed primary responsibility on local school officials to integrate schools. Federal district courts were to retain jurisdiction over school desegregation cases. They could give school districts additional time to complete desegregation after the process was begun, but only if school boards could prove that such delays were necessary.

A violent reaction to the *Brown* decisions occurred in Little Rock, Arkansas, in 1958. School officials there had developed a plan to gradually desegregate the city's schools. But, as a result of a statewide referendum in which the voters turned down school integration, the state legislature enacted a law permitting children in racially mixed schools to ignore compulsory attendance rules. This meant, in effect, that students could not be compelled to attend integrated schools. When nine black students attempted to

Thurgood Marshall, who as NAACP chief counsel argued the
Brown v. *Board of Education* case before the High Court, and Daisy
Bates, head of the Little Rock chapter of the NAACP, are seen with
six of the first African-American children to attend Central High
School in Little Rock, Arkansas.

enroll at all-white Central High School in Little Rock, Governor Orval Faubus called out the state national guard to block their entry. President Dwight D. Eisenhower then sent federal troops to protect black students when they enrolled at Central High School and also when they attended its classes.

In response to the public hostility generated by this incident, the Little Rock school board requested permission from the district court to remove the black students from the high school and to postpone any further desegregation for two and one half years. The district court agreed to this request, but an appeals court overturned this ruling. When the school board appealed to the Supreme Court in *Cooper* v. *Aaron,* the justices voted unanimously that the black students must be admitted to Central High School, that it was unconstitutional for the Arkansas legislature to deny black students the equal protection of the laws, and that it would not tolerate any state action continuing segregation in the Arkansas public schools.

Prince Edward County, a rural county in Virginia, tried a different maneuver to avoid desegregation—it closed its public schools. White children thereafter attended private schools, partially funded by contributions from individuals and partially financed by public funds. The county offered to set up similar schools for African Americans, but they refused the offer and filed a lawsuit demanding integrated public schools.

When this case of *Griffin* v. *Prince Edward County* reached the Supreme Court in 1964, the Court, by a 7 to 2 margin, ruled against the county's closure of public schools. Justice Black, writing for the majority, said, "There has been entirely too much deliberation and not enough speed in enforcing the constitutional rights which we held in *Brown.*" The Warren Court decreed that private schools could not be maintained in part by public funds when public schools are closed and that the federal district court must order Prince Edward officials to reopen and finance racially desegregated schools.

Although the High Court at first limited its integration orders to schools, Court analyst Richard Kluger observed that "it became almost immediately clear that Brown had in effect wiped out all forms of state-sanctioned segregation."[5] Congress passed major civil rights acts in 1964, 1965, and 1968. The Civil Rights Act of 1964 outlawed discrimination in public accommodations (such as restaurants, hotels, and other facilities open to the public), forbade employment discrimination and set up an Equal Opportunity Commission, authorized the Department of Justice to file lawsuits to facilitate school integration, and prohibited segregation in federally funded projects. The Voting Rights Act of 1965 empowered the federal government to suspend all literacy and other tests for voting in areas where less than half of the adults were registered to vote, and permitted the national government to send registrars to supervise the enrollment of voters in areas that previously had denied the vote to African Americans or other minorities. The Civil Rights Act of 1968 prohibited discrimination in the sale and rental of housing.

All three of these acts were challenged in the courts, and the decisions of the lower courts were appealed to the Supreme Court. In all three instances, the Warren Court upheld the constitutionality of the civil rights acts passed by Congress.

LEGACY OF THE BURGER COURT

The first desegregation case that reached the Burger Court was *Alexander* v. *Holmes Board of Education* in 1969. The case involved a request from thirty-three Mississippi school districts that they be granted an indefinite delay in desegregating their public schools. The case took on added significance because officials in the administration of President Richard M. Nixon argued in favor of permitting the delay. (Nixon had won the presidency in 1968 in part because of support from southern voters, and he believed that one way to establish a strong Republican base in the South was to assure southerners that he wanted to slow down the integration of public schools).

The Burger Court voted unanimously to deny the school districts' request for a delay in desegregating their schools. The Court declared that the previous standard of integrating schools with "all deliberate speed" was "no longer constitutionally permissible"—fifteen years after *Brown*—and ordered the school districts to begin immediate operation of integrated schools.

In the 1971 case of *Swann* v. *Charlotte-Mecklenburg County*

Board of Education, decided by a unanimous vote, the Supreme Court ruled that school officials could use various methods to achieve desegregation. These methods could include the busing of students, the racial balancing of schools by establishing a ratio of black students to white students, and the redrawing of boundaries of school districts to promote integration. But Chief Justice Warren E. Burger, writing the Court opinion, said that "the constitutional command to desegregate schools does not mean that every school in every community must always reflect the racial composition of the school system as a whole."

In subsequent school desegregation cases, the Burger Court continued to uphold *Brown,* but it struck down desegregation plans that it considered unreasonable. By a vote of 5 to 4, the Court in 1974 reversed a district court plan to integrate schools in Detroit, Michigan, by busing students among fifty-four school districts in three counties. The Court majority asserted that this plan was too drastic since it had not been proved that all fifty-four districts had been guilty of segregation. In a 1976 case, the Court ruled, by a 6 to 2 vote, that once a school board had established a racially neutral plan for assignment of students to city schools, it is not constitutionally required to continue juggling student enrollments in order to maintain a specific racial balance in the student body of each school.

The Supreme Court decided a landmark case in 1978 that pertained to "reverse discrimination." It dealt with the question of whether white persons are discriminated against when certain actions are taken to improve the status of racial minorities— actions that could adversely affect white citizens. President Lyndon B. Johnson in 1965 had issued executive orders calling for businesses to create more jobs and universities more educational opportunities for minorities and women. Described as "affirmative action," these orders were intended to help African Americans and others that were handicapped by existing discrimination and the effects of past discrimination. Many employers and educational institutions then began opening more doors to the disadvantaged. The medical school of the University of California at Davis was one of the educational institutions that developed an affirmative action plan to ensure more minority representation in its student body. Among the one hundred new students it enrolled each year, the Davis medical school set aside sixteen openings for "economically and educationally disadvantaged minority students."

Alan Bakke, a white, was twice denied admission to the Davis medical school. In each year that Bakke's application had been rejected, the school did accept some minority students with qualifications inferior to his. Bakke filed suit, charging that the Davis "quota system" for minorities violated the California Constitution, the equal protection clause of the Fourteenth Amendment, and Title VI of the Civil Rights Act of 1964. A California superior court judge ruled that the Davis admissions policy was invalid because it discriminated against Bakke. When the school appealed the case to the California Supreme Court, it declared that Davis's use of affirmative action was unconstitutional because it deprived whites of the equal protection of their rights. The medical school was ordered to admit Bakke, but the Davis officials appealed the case to the Supreme Court.

Two important questions needed to be resolved in the Bakke case: Did the medical school violate a white applicant's rights by denying him admission, even though his qualifications for enrollment were higher than those of some minority applicants who were admitted? Were affirmative action programs designed to improve the status of minorities constitutional? The Burger Court responded to these questions by rendering two separate decisions, each by a vote of 5 to 4. Justice Lewis F. Powell, Jr., was the swing voter in both decisions.

Powell agreed with four other members of the Court—Chief Justice Burger and Justices Rehnquist, Stewart, and Stevens—that Bakke's rights had been violated and he must be admitted to the Davis medical school. However, Powell's reason for taking this position was different from that of his four colleagues who had also voted in Bakke's favor; he contended that the school had erred because its admission policy denied equal protection of the laws and thus was unconstitutional. The other four justices in the majority maintained that Bakke's rights had been violated under Title VI of the 1964 Civil Rights Act and that racial quotas such as those used at Davis were illegal. In the words of Justice Stevens, the Civil Rights Act "required a colorblind standard on the part of the government. . . . Under Title VI it is not permissible to say 'yes' to one person, but to say 'no' to another person, only because of the color of his skin."

In the second Bakke decision, Powell joined four other justices—Brennan, Marshall, Blackmun, and White—in approving the use of affirmative action programs to reduce discrimination. The Court majority held that admission officers can consider race as one of several factors that determine which applicant is accepted and which rejected.

Both sides won partial victories in this case. Bakke was granted the right to enter the Davis medical school, which he did. At the same time, affirmative action programs were upheld as constitutional, but the establishment of specific racial quotas was struck down.

Later, the Burger Court decided other important civil rights cases. It ruled in 1979 that employers may adopt affirmative action programs to encourage minority participation in areas of work in which minorities traditionally have not been fairly represented. In 1983, the Court decided that the Internal Revenue Service had acted within its authority when it denied tax-exempt status to private schools that discriminate against African Americans.

Officials in the administration of President Reagan strongly opposed most affirmative action programs, which they regarded as "reverse discrimination, penalizing innocent whites— usually white men—for past discrimination by others against blacks and women."6 The first two affirmative action cases heard by the Supreme Court during the Reagan presidency chipped away at programs that had been used to protect the jobs of more recently hired blacks at the cost of white employees who had longer seniority. In a 1984 ruling, decided by a 6 to 3 vote, the Court declared that a federal judge could not strike down a valid seniority system set up by a firefighters' union because it conflicted with an affirmative action plan to preserve the jobs of black workers. Two years later, the Court voted 5 to 4 that it was unconstitutional for a school board to adopt an affirmative action program under which white teachers with more seniority were laid off to protect the jobs of black teachers with less seniority. In both of these cases, the Court majority said that the affirmative action program denied white employees the equal protection of the laws.

THE REHNQUIST COURT

In 1987, shortly after William H. Rehnquist became chief justice, the Supreme Court voted 5 to 4 to uphold a federal judge's decree that Alabama must promote one black state police officer for every white police officer promoted in order to help remedy the state's long-standing discrimination against African Americans. Rehnquist was a dissenter in this case, but after the 1988 appointment of Anthony M. Kennedy to the High Court, the chief justice's conservative viewpoint usually triumphed in cases pertaining to affirmative action.

The Court considered in 1989 a plan adopted by the city council of Richmond, Virginia, requiring that at least 30 percent of city funds for construction projects be given to minority-owned firms. By a 6 to 3 vote, the Rehnquist Court struck down the Richmond plan on the grounds that it violated the constitutional rights of whites, was too rigid, and was not justified by a clear history of specific discrimination in the past.

Another 1989 case involved mostly Filipino workers at an Alaskan salmon cannery who had filed a discrimination suit in which they asserted that nonwhites were largely excluded from higher-paying, skilled jobs. Their attorneys presented statistics showing that most of the Filipino employees held lower-paying jobs. The company lawyers argued that the cannery had not intentionally discriminated against any racial or ethnic group of workers and that its promotion standards were based entirely on its business needs. Voting 5 to 4, the Court decided in favor of the cannery and established this new legal precedent: minority employees may not rely on statistics alone to prove that job policies are discriminatory; employers need show only a legitimate business reason for their promotion policies in order to disprove bias. Justice Blackmun, one of the dissenters, wrote bitterly, "One wonders whether the majority still believes that race discrimination—or, more accurately, race discrimination against nonwhites—is a problem in our society, or even remembers that it ever was."

White firefighters in Birmingham, Alabama, contested the city's affirmative action plan, claiming that it represented reverse discrimination. In its 5 to 4 decision in *Martin* v. *Wilks* (1989), the Rehnquist Court sided with the white firefighters and sent the case back to a trial judge in Birmingham, with orders to hear the claims of this group that was challenging an earlier court-approved affirmative action program.

Justice White had voted with conservative justices on most previous affirmative action cases decided by the Rehnquist Court. But in 1990, he temporarily parted company with the Rehnquist bloc and provided the fifth vote in a case that upheld the federal government's right to give preferences to minorities in certain instances. Since 1978, the Federal Communications Commission (FCC) had given a preference to minority-owned companies in the competition for new broadcast licenses. (At that time, although minorities made up 20 percent of the U.S. population, they controlled fewer than 1 percent of the nation's television and radio stations.)[7] In 1988, the FCC awarded the license of a new television station in Florida to Rainbow Broadcasting Company, owned by Hispanics, instead of to Metro Broadcasting Company, which was controlled by whites. Metro then filed suit, claiming that its owners had been subjected to reverse discrimination.

The 5 to 4 vote by the Supreme Court in favor of the Hispanic station was applauded by civil rights groups. Delivering his last opinion before his retirement from the Court, Justice Brennan said, "We hold today that benign [harmless] race-conscious measures . . . are constitutionally permissible!"

In dissent, Justice Kennedy criticized the Court for "its assumed role of case-by-case arbiter of when it is desirable and benign for the Government to disfavor some citizens and favor others based on the color of skin."

The Supreme Court in 1992 decided a civil rights case in which the charge of racial discrimination was the chief factor. The case was based on a trial in which a black couple claimed that three white persons had assaulted them in Albany, Georgia, a city with a 43 percent black population. Lawyers for the defendants tried to reject potential black jurors in an attempt to obtain an all-white jury. Traditionally, defense attorneys are allowed to exclude, without any explanation, a fixed number of potential jurors from serving in a trial. But in this situation it became apparent that all prospective African-American jurors were being excluded because they were black.

By a 7 to 2 vote, the Supreme Court decreed that defendants' lawyers cannot reject people from juries because of their race. "Be it at the hands of the state or the defense," wrote Justice Blackmun for the majority, "if a court allows jurors to be excluded because of group bias, it is a willing participant in a scheme that could only undermine the very foundation of our system of justice—our citizens' confidence in it." The two dissenters were Justices O'Connor and Scalia. In her dissent, O'Connor expressed the fear that this Court decision would have an adverse effect on black defendants who want to exclude potential white jurors in order to get minority representation on their juries.

In its first major case dealing with higher-education racial discrimination, the Rehnquist Court in 1992 had to decide whether the state of Mississippi had done enough to dismantle its formerly segregated system of public colleges and universities. State officials argued that they had opened their institutions of higher learning to all students regardless of race and were spending almost as much money on black college students as white ones.

Civil rights advocates said that these steps had not been sufficient to overcome the state's long history of enforced segregation at the college level. Figures showed that in 1986 nearly 99 percent of the state's white college students were enrolled at one of five historically white campuses, while 71 percent of its black students attended predominantly black colleges. African Americans charged that Mississippi had fostered segregation in part by basing admission to the state's predominantly white colleges chiefly on standardized tests that discriminated against many black students who had attended inferior elementary and secondary schools.

This case, *United States* v. *Fordice,* was decided by a vote of 8 to 1, with Justice Scalia the lone dissenter. The Supreme Court ruled that the Mississippi system of higher education "may not leave in place policies rooted in its prior officially segregated system." Writing for the majority, Justice White said Mississippi had wrongly designated its white colleges as "flagship institutions" that received the most money and offered the most advanced courses. The Court ordered a federal trial judge to reopen a lawsuit filed against Mississippi officials and review policies, including admissions tests, that have slowed integration in the state's colleges and universities.

While the two major civil rights cases decided by the Rehnquist Court in 1992 upheld the claims of African Americans, the most important 1993 cases in this area provided setbacks for minority groups. In one case decided by a 5 to 4 vote, the Court made it more difficult for workers charging discrimination to prevail against their employers. Previously, a worker was likely to win a discrimination case if an employer was unable to prove in court that there were other legitimate reasons for firing the employee. As a result of the Court's ruling in this case, the worker now has to prove that the actual reason for being dismissed is intentional bias on the part of the employer. Thus, the Court has shifted the burden of proof in discrimination cases from the employer to the employee.

Perhaps the most significant 1993 civil rights case involved the practice of gerrymandering, which is the drawing of legislative district boundary lines in an irregular way. (The term *gerrymander* originated in the early 1800s to describe a salamander-shaped district engineered by Massachusetts governor Elbridge Gerry.) In North Carolina, about 22 percent of the state population is black, but the state had sent no African Americans to the House of Representatives in the twentieth century. So in 1991 the North Carolina legislature redrew the boundary lines of congressional districts to include two districts that had more black than white residents. The following year, voters elected African-American representatives from these two districts.

North Carolina's Twelfth District had been redrawn in a bizarre manner to ensure that it would encompass an area in which blacks outnumbered whites. Stretching some 160 miles from north to south, but often no wider than the two lanes of an interstate highway, it excluded many whites while including a 53 percent black majority. Five white voters then filed a suit claiming that the gerrymandering of the Twelfth District violated their equal protection of the laws.

The Supreme Court voted 5 to 4 in this case (*Shaw* v. *Reno*) that North Carolina's legislature had violated the constitutional provision of equal treatment for all when it drew the boundaries of the Twelfth District. Expressing the opinion of the majority, Justice O'Connor stated that it was not constitutionally permissible to draw district boundaries that are "highly irregular" and "can be viewed only as an effort to segregate the races for purposes of voting." The Court's ruling raised the important question of whether any states could constitutionally establish districts along racial or ethnic lines to ensure greater representation of minorities in Congress.

O'Connor was joined in the majority by Chief Justice Rehnquist and Justices Scalia, Kennedy, and Thomas. The minority consisted of Justices White, Stevens, Blackmun, and Souter. In his final dissent before retiring from the Court, White said that it was "both a fiction and a departure from settled equal-protection principles" for the majority to assert that North Carolina had erred in creating new electoral districts intended to help blacks gain seats in Congress. Stevens, in a separate dissent, declared, "If it is permissible to draw boundaries to provide adequate representation for rural voters, for union members . . . it necessarily follows that it is permissible to do the same thing for members of the very minority group whose history in the United States gave birth to the Equal Protection Clause."

Another civil rights case pertaining to minority representation in a legislative body was decided by the Rehnquist Court in 1994. A Florida judge, basing his action on the Voting Rights Act of 1965, had ordered the redistricting of the state's House of Representatives in order to create the greatest possible number of districts in which Hispanic voters would make up a majority. This lower-court order called for the number of Hispanic-majority districts in Dade County, Florida, to be increased from nine to eleven, out of a total of twenty. Hispanics constitute about 45 percent of the Dade County population.

Voting 7 to 2, the Supreme Court overturned the judge's redistricting plan. Speaking for the majority, Justice Souter explained that when a minority group has achieved representation in rough proportion to its population, there is ordinarily no reason to go further. Referring to the nine Hispanic-majority districts already created in Dade County, Souter said, ". . . we do not see how these district lines, apparently providing political effectiveness in proportion to voting-age numbers, deny equal political opportunity."

ABORTION

Abortion has been commonly accepted in large areas of the world for many years and practiced in North America even before the founding of the United States. Since colonial days, Americans have considered abortion primarily as a means of dealing with unwanted pregnancies caused by illicit relationships and rape. When doctors estimated American abortion rates in the 1860s and 1870s, they produced figures strikingly similar to those of the 1960s and 1970s: approximately one abortion for every four live births.[1] In the 1990s, about 1.6 million abortions occur every year in the United States.

Some state legislatures began to restrict abortions in the second half of the nineteenth century. At that time, abortion was a very risky operation, often fatal. Antiabortion laws were enacted mainly to protect the health of pregnant women. In states that made abortion a crime, illegal operations continued to be performed, even though they were driven underground.

By the 1960s, many people began calling for repeal of the abortion restrictions. Modern medical procedures had eliminated most of the operation's risks—at least in the early months of pregnancy. As the feminist movement came to the forefront in the 1960s and 1970s, millions of Americans demanded that women should have control of their own bodies, including the right to terminate (end) unwanted pregnancies. Arguing that pregnant women, not the government, should have the power to decide whether they give birth, abortion advocates adopted what became known as a "pro-choice" position. Millions of other Americans asserted that human life begins with conception and that destroying a fetus (unborn child) is an act of murder. Opponents of abortion adopted what was called a "pro-life" stance.

During the past few decades, pro-choice and pro-life forces have engaged in bitter and sometimes bloody warfare. The issue of abortion has become one of the most heated controversies in modern society.

LEGACY OF THE WARREN COURT

There is no mention of abortion in the Constitution, including its amendments, and the Warren Court heard no cases on this issue. However, an important case pertaining to privacy was decided by the Warren Court, and it provided the cornerstone for consideration of abortion cases by the Burger Court.

A Connecticut law forbade the use of contraceptives, even by married couples, and further specified that any person who assisted another in committing this offense could also be prosecuted and punished. Enacted in the nineteenth century, this law was frequently violated and seldom enforced, but supporters of family planning and civil rights advocates were eager to contest it in the courts. The opportunity for a legal challenge came after the arrest and conviction of Estelle Griswold, the executive director of the Planned Parenthood League of Connecticut, who had given information and advice on birth control measures to married persons. Her conviction was upheld by an appellate court and by Connecticut's supreme court.

In 1965 the Warren Court, by a vote of 7 to 2, overturned Griswold's conviction and struck down the Connecticut law as an unconstitutional invasion of people's privacy—even though nothing is said about privacy in the Constitution's Bill of Rights. Writing for the majority, Justice William O. Douglas asserted that in the case of *Griswold* v. *Connecticut*, ". . . we deal with a right of privacy older than the Bill of Rights." Douglas maintained that the First, Fourth, Fifth, and Ninth amendments all imply that the right of privacy is legitimate. He especially emphasized the inclusion of privacy as part of the Ninth Amendment, which states that "the enumeration in the Constitution, of certain rights, shall not be construed to deny or disparage other rights retained by the people."

Justices Stewart and Black opposed the majority decision. Stewart conceded that the Connecticut statute was an "uncommonly silly law," but he said it was not on that account unconstitutional. This conservative justice reminded his colleagues that courts should not "substitute their social and economic beliefs for the judgment of legislative bodies, who are elected to pass laws." In his dissent, Justice Black held that subjecting laws to unrestrained judicial control would "jeopardize the separation of governmental powers that the framers set up and at the same time threaten to take away much of the power of States to govern themselves which the Constitution plainly intended them to have."

LEGACY OF THE BURGER COURT

A Texas law prohibited all abortions except under extreme conditions when a doctor certified that this medical procedure was necessary to save the life of the woman. Challenging this restrictive law, a pregnant woman filed a lawsuit that was known as *Roe* v. *Wade*. (Roe was a fictitious name to protect the woman's identity; Wade was the district attorney of Dallas County.)

When *Roe* v. *Wade* reached the Supreme Court in 1973, it attracted nationwide attention, since the Court's decision would determine the legality of abortions not only in Texas, but throughout the country. By a 7 to 2 vote, the Burger Court overturned the Texas law banning abortion. Justice Blackmun wrote the majority opinion. "The Constitution does not explicitly mention any right of privacy," he admitted. "However, . . . the Court has recognized that a right of personal privacy, or a guarantee of certain areas or zones of privacy, does exist under the Constitution." He pointed to the Fourteenth Amendment's concept of personal liberty and the Ninth Amendment's reservation of rights to the people as the chief sources for the right of privacy.

But whatever the source, Blackmun declared, "this right of privacy . . . is broad enough to encompass a woman's decision whether or not to terminate her pregnancy."

Blackmun added, however, that the right to an abortion is not an absolute right; there are times, he said, when the state "may properly assert important interests" in preventing abortions. To help define these times when the government may restrict abortions, Blackmun, speaking for the Court majority, laid down specific regulations pertaining to the different stages of pregnancy. In the first trimester (three months of pregnancy), a woman may decide without any state interference whether she will have an abortion. In the second trimester, when a woman is more likely to be physically harmed by an abortion, the state has a compelling interest in protecting her and could therefore regulate the abortion procedure by requiring, for example, that it be performed in a hospital. In the third trimester, when the fetus probably could live on its own outside the mother's body, the state's compelling interest becomes the protection of the life of the fetus. To protect the fetus during the final three months of pregnancy, Blackmun concluded, the state can enact laws forbidding abortions, except in instances where the operation is necessary to protect the life or health of the mother.

The two dissenting justices in *Roe* v. *Wade* were White and Rehnquist. "The Court," White wrote, "apparently values the convenience of the pregnant mother more than the continued existence and development of the life or potential life that she carries." In Rehnquist's dissent, he questioned Blackmun's claim that the Fourteenth Amendment was a legitimate source for extending the so-called right of privacy to include abortions. Rehnquist pointed out that in 1868, when the Fourteenth Amendment was adopted, at least thirty-six states or U.S. territories had laws limit-

Warren Burger was chief justice when the Supreme Court handed down one of its most controversial rulings, that in the *Roe* v. *Wade* case.

ing abortion. Therefore, he asserted, it did not appear that the framers of the Fourteenth Amendment intended to prohibit the states from regulating abortions or they would have mentioned this subject in their amendment.

Roe v. *Wade* was the most controversial decision handed down by the Burger Court. It caused a deluge of mail, telegrams, and phone calls to flood the justices' offices. Pro-choice forces applauded the Court's judgment that women could control their reproductive processes; pro-life adherents, led by the Roman Catholic Church, labeled the Court's decision a death sentence for unborn children. "How many millions of children prior to their birth will never live to see the light of day because of the shocking action of the majority of the United States Supreme Court today?" asked Catholic prelate Terence Cardinal Cooke of New York.[2]

John Joseph Cardinal Krol of Philadelphia, the president of the National Council of Catholic Bishops, was appalled by the Court ruling. "It is hard to think of any decision in the two hundred years of our history," he said, "which has had more disastrous implications for our stability as a civilized society."[3]

While the Burger Court ruled in favor of women who sought abortions, it decreed in 1980 that Congress could restrict federal funding of these operations. The Court upheld the Hyde Amendment, adopted by Congress in 1976, which denies federal financing for abortions under the Medicaid program except when the abortion is necessary to save the pregnant woman's life or to terminate a pregnancy caused by promptly reported rape or incest.

Shortly before Chief Justice Burger resigned from the bench in 1986, the Supreme Court dealt with another major abortion case. It involved a Pennsylvania law designed to discourage women from having abortions. This law required physicians to tell a pregnant woman considering abortion about the possibility that harmful physical and psychological effects could be caused by the abortion procedure. The doctor also had to give the woman information about agencies that could assist her if she decided to give birth, and about the physical characteristics of the unborn child at two-week intervals.

By a 5 to 4 vote in *Thornburgh* v. *American College of*

Obstetricians and Gynecologists, the Burger Court reaffirmed *Roe* v. *Wade* and struck down the Pennsylvania law. Justice Blackmun, who had written the Court's *Roe* opinion, again spoke for the majority. "The states are not free," Blackmun maintained, "under the guise of protecting maternal health or potential life, to intimidate women into continuing pregnancies."

Dissenting justice White accused the Court majority of defining "fundamental" liberties "that are nowhere mentioned in the Constitution." White asserted that instead of imposing "its own controversial choices of value[s] on the people," the Court should allow the state legislatures to express the will of the public on such strongly debated moral and political issues.

Court observers pointed to the difference between the margin of votes in the *Roe* and *Thornburgh* cases. While seven justices had voted for *Roe* in 1973, thirteen years later only five justices cast pro-choice votes in *Thornburgh*. The appointment to the Court of just one more pro-life justice might tip the scales in favor of striking down *Roe* and returning the entire abortion issue to the states.

THE REHNQUIST COURT

Ronald Reagan, who served as president from 1981 to 1989, was strongly opposed to abortion, so when he had the opportunity to fill vacancies on the Supreme Court he sought nominees who shared his philosophy. Sandra Day O'Connor, whom Reagan named to the High Court in 1981, had been critical of the *Roe* decision, even though she never stated that all abortions should be prohibited. Following the resignation of Chief Justice Burger in 1986, President Reagan made two Supreme Court appointments. He elevated Justice Rehnquist (one of two justices who had dissented in *Roe* v. *Wade*) to the position of chief justice and selected Antonin Scalia, also critical of *Roe*, to replace Rehnquist. In 1988, when Justice Powell resigned, Reagan appointed Anthony M. Kennedy, a Roman Catholic and presumably an opponent of abortion rights, to the High Court.

The Rehnquist Court heard its first major abortion case, *Webster* v. *Reproductive Health Services,* in 1989. At that time five Court members were considered antiabortionists, and there was a strong possibility that legal abortions, which had been permitted for sixteen years since the *Roe* ruling, would be struck down. The *Webster* case stemmed from a Missouri law that banned abortions in any public hospital and prohibted the distribution of public funds for abortion services. Furthermore, the Missouri law required doctors to test for the viability of a fetus (its capability to live outside the womb) at twenty weeks, or two thirds of the way through the second trimester of pregnancy.

Pro-life advocates rejoiced and pro-choice supporters were angered when the Court voted 5 to 4 to uphold the Missouri law. President Reagan's four Court appointees plus Justice White, a dissenter from *Roe,* constituted the majority in this important case. While the Rehnquist Court did not reverse *Roe* outright, its willingness to approve a ban on abortions in publicly funded hospitals and tests for fetal viability past the midpoint of pregnancy was widely viewed as a step toward repudiation of Roe. Harvard law professor Laurence Tribe interpreted the *Webster* decision as "burning the heart out of *Roe* v. *Wade.*"[4]

This Court ruling signaled state governments that the door now was open to further restrictions on abortions. "The rigid *Roe* framework is hardly consistent with the notion of a Constitution case," argued Chief Justice Rehnquist in his majority opinion. He added, "We do not see why the state's interest in protecting human life should come into existence only at the point of [fetal] viability, and that there should therefore be a rigid line allowing state regulation [of abortion] after viability but prohibiting it before viability."

Justice Scalia was disappointed that Webster had not completely overturned *Roe.* This case, he observed, "preserves a chaos to anyone who can read and count." He said, "We can now look forward to at least another term with carts full of mail . . . and streets full of demonstrators urging us . . . to follow the popular will . . . ." (Public opinion polls in 1989 showed a majority of Americans favoring legalized abortion but also favoring some restrictions on this procedure.)

In his dissenting opinion, Justice Blackmun expressed the fear that the *Webster* decision left *Roe* hanging by only a slender thread. It "is filled with winks and nods and knowing glances to those who would do away with *Roe* explicitly," he wrote. "The signs of change," he continued, "are evident and very ominous, and a chill wind blows."

In 1990, the Rehnquist Court dealt with two cases involving abortion regulations imposed on pregnant teenagers. A Minnesota law required that both parents of a pregnant minor be notified if she sought an abortion. Voting 5 to 4, the justices struck down this law on the grounds that one parent might be absent or abusive. Speaking for the majority, Justice Stevens said that in the "ideal family setting" a minor's notice to either parent would normally constitute notice to both, but the state should not presume that any one parent is incompetent to provide for a daughter's well-being. In the same case, however, a different majority of five (Justice O'Connor cast the swing vote) upheld a so-called "judicial bypass" of the law, under which a pregnant teenager who will not or cannot tell both parents must obtain a court order permitting her doctor to proceed with the abortion.

Justice Kennedy was one of the four Court members who dissented from that part of the decision which overturned the requirement that both parents be notified before a teenager could obtain an abortion. State abortion restrictions on minors, he contended, "rest upon a tradition of a parental role in the care and upbringing of children that is as old as civilization itself."

The other 1990 case arose from a 1985 Ohio abortion law that required a pregnant minor to persuade a judge by "clear and convincing evidence" that she is mature enough to decide to have an abortion without notifying either parent. By a margin of 6 to 3, the Court voted to uphold the Ohio law. Justice Kennedy, again siding with the right-to-life advocates, wrote the majority opinion. For a minor woman "who is considering whether to seek an abortion," Kennedy said, "her decision will embrace her own destiny and personal dignity, and the origins of the other human life that lie within the embryo. . . . It would deny all dignity to the family to say that the State cannot take this reasonable step . . . to ensure that, in most cases, a young woman will receive guidance and understanding from a parent."

George Bush became president in 1989, and, like Ronald

Reagan, his predecessor in the White House, he was an opponent of abortion. In 1990, liberal justice William J. Brennan, Jr., retired from the Supreme Court, and President Bush replaced him with moderately conservative David H. Souter. The following year, Thurgood Marshall, another liberal, retired, and the vacancy was filled by the appointment of conservative Clarence Thomas. After Brennan and Marshall stepped down from the bench, there remained only two justices who could be counted on to vote for the preservation of abortion rights—Harry A. Blackmun and John Paul Stevens. Most Court observers predicted that *Roe* v. *Wade* would not survive the next major abortion case heard by the justices.

This test came in 1992 when the important case of *Planned Parenthood of Southeastern Pennsylvania* v. *Casey* was decided. It was based on a 1989 Pennsylvania law that imposed stringent regulations on the abortion procedure. The strongest Court foes of abortion, led by Chief Justice Rehnquist, were determined to use this case as the vehicle for overturning *Roe* v. *Wade* entirely, thus permitting states to outlaw all abortions. Rehnquist's viewpoint had strong support from the executive department of the government. Repeatedly, attorneys for the Reagan and Bush administrations had urged the Court to strike down *Roe*, and U.S. Solicitor Kenneth W. Starr did so again when he appeared before the justices to argue the Pennsylvania case.

Right-to-life advocates applauded the many abortion restrictions and regulations in the Pennsylvania law. It required that the pregnant woman certify in writing that she had been warned of the risks involved in abortions, be told the age of the fetus, and be informed by her doctor about alternatives to abortion, such as adoption. Except for medical emergencies, the doctor was to wait twenty-four hours after conferring with the pregnant woman before performing the abortion procedure. The law stated that these regulations were imposed to help ensure that a pregnant woman make an "informed choice."

The Pennsylvania law also required that a pregnant minor get the consent of one parent or approval from a judge before having an abortion. Abortion clinics were to maintain records on the procedures performed and report certain information, including the names of referring physicians, so long as the identity of the patients was kept confidential. Finally, the law required a married woman to submit a signed statement that she had notified her husband of her intention to have an abortion.

The Rehnquist Court voted 5 to 4 to uphold all the provisions of the Pennsylvania law except one; it struck down the requirement that a woman notify her husband before having an abortion. That provision posed an "undue burden" on the woman, the Court majority said, because "for the great many women who are victims of abuse inflicted by their husbands," notifying the spouse enables him "to wield an effective veto over his wife's decision." However, the most astonishing part of the decision in this case was that the Court majority reaffirmed *Roe* v. *Wade* and the basic right of women to have abortions. This happened because three of the justices—O'Connor, Souter, and Kennedy—deserted their more conservative colleagues and took a moderate stance in which they approved most of the Pennsylvania law but refused to overturn *Roe*. The most surprising member of this trio was Kennedy, who had taken the right-to-life position in previous abortion cases.

Justices O'Connor, Souter, and Kennedy shared the writing of the majority opinion, which was also signed by Justices Blackmun and Stevens. "A state may not prohibit any woman from making the ultimate decision to terminate her pregnancy before viability," O'Connor wrote. "The central holding of *Roe* v. *Wade* must be reaffirmed. . . . Some of us as individuals find abortion offensive to our most basic principles of morality, but that cannot control our decision," O'Connor continued. "Our obligation is to define the liberty of all, not to mandate our own moral code."

Souter emphasized the importance of adhering to a Court precedent, even one that was highly controversial. "An entire generation has come of age free to assume *Roe*'s concept of liberty in defining the capacity of women . . . to make reproductive decisions," he said, and to overthrow *Roe* now would undermine "the legitimacy of the Court."

Kennedy asserted that the Constitution creates a "realm of personal liberty which the government may not enter. . . . At the heart of liberty is the right to define one's own concept of

The 1973 *Roe* v. *Wade* ruling on a woman's right to an abortion caused heated demonstrations—both for and against abortion—all across the nation.

existence, of meaning, of the universe and of the mystery of human life."

Pleased that three generally conservative justices had taken a moderate position on abortion, Blackmun exclaimed that "just when so many expected the darkness to fall, the flame has grown bright. Make no mistake, the joint opinion of Justices O'Connor, Kennedy and Souter is an act of personal courage and constitutional principle."

The four justices in the minority on this landmark case—Rehnquist, White, Scalia, and Thomas—were deeply disappointed by the decision. Rehnquist, in one of two dissents, insisted that *Roe* "was wrongly decided" in 1973 and "should be overruled." In the other dissent, Scalia attacked the majority for imposing "a rigid national rule [permitting abortion] instead of allowing regional differences."

Subsequent Court abortion decisions generally followed the framework established by the Pennsylvania case. By a 6 to 3 vote in 1992, the Court overturned a 1990 Guam law that banned nearly all abortions. But in another 1992 case, the Court refused to interfere with a Mississippi law requiring a doctor to offer a woman counseling on alternatives to abortion and then to wait twenty-four hours before performing the procedure. A similar twenty-four-hour waiting period in North Dakota was upheld by a 7 to 2 vote in 1993.

The abortion debate continued to inflame the public, and huge demonstrations by both sides were staged throughout the country. One antiabortion group, called Operation Rescue, launched human blockades of abortion clinics to try to prevent women and doctors from entering the clinics. Sometimes these confrontations between pro-life and pro-choice forces turned violent. Judges in various cities issued orders to stop Operation Rescue's clinic blockades and acts of violence that were occurring. The judges based their orders on the Civil Rights Act of 1871, also known as the Ku Klux Klan Act, which had been enacted to protect blacks from white mobs (often led by the racist Klan organization) in the South in the years after the Civil War. This law authorized judges to intervene "if two or more persons conspire" to use force to prevent others from exercising "any right or privilege" under the Constitution.

The Rehnquist Court had to decide in 1993 whether the nineteenth-century Ku Klux Klan Act could be applied to stop physical attacks motivated by abortion opponents. In a 6 to 3 decision, the Court ruled that this law could not be used by judges who sought to intervene by restraining abortion clinic blockades and acts of violence. Speaking for the majority, Justice Scalia explained that the actions of pro-life groups could not be compared to the ruthless, racially motivated attacks waged by the Ku Klux Klan. "Whether one agrees or disagrees with the goal of preventing abortion," he said, "that goal in itself does not remotely qualify for such harsh description [as racial hatred] and for such derogatory association with racism. . . Whatever one thinks of abortion, it cannot be denied that there are common and respectable reasons for opposing it. . . ."

The minority opinion, signed by Justices O'Connor, Stevens, and Blackmun, argued that Operation Rescue's use of "organized and violent mobs . . . presents a striking contemporary example of the kind of zealous, politically motivated, lawless conduct that led to the Ku Klux Klan Act in 1871."

Appalled when an abortion doctor was slain by an antiabortion activist in 1993, abortion supporters searched for another law to use against their foes. They decided to wage a court battle based on the Racketeer Influenced and Corrupt Organizations (RICO) Act of 1970. This law was originally applied against conspiracies of racketeers and other mobsters who committed crimes against businesses. It penalties are steep: up to twenty years in prison for each criminal count and damage payments three times greater than the total losses suffered by the victims. The National Organization for Women (NOW) sued two pro-life groups, claiming that they were racketeering conspiracies engaged in extortion (using improper pressure) by means of abortion clinic blockades, assaults, bombings, arson, break-ins, and threats.

Both a federal district court and the Seventh Circuit Court of Appeals ruled against NOW on the grounds that RICO requires that racketeering must be for economic motives and the actions of pro-life groups were motivated by moral reasons. In 1994, the

Supreme Court unanimously reversed the lower courts' decisions. Chief Justice Rehnquist declared that "nowhere in [RICO] is there any indication that an economic motive is required." He explained that a group sued under the RICO provisions "need only be an association in fact that engages in a pattern of racketeering activity."

Pro-choice leaders also sought new legislation to curb extremist activities practiced by some of their opponents. They claimed that between 1977 and early 1993 right-to-life terrorists were responsible for 36 bombings, 81 cases of arson, 84 assaults, 131 death threats, and the slaying of Dr. David Gunn in Florida in March 1993.

Congress responded by passsing a bill in 1994 prohibiting abortion clinic blockades and making it a crime to engage in threats or violence against the clinics, their staffs, and the women who used the clinics. Nonviolent blocking of a clinic entrance would be punishable by as much as six months in prison and a fine of up to $10,000. First offenders who committed violent acts could be sent to prison for up to one year and made to pay fines ranging up to $100,000. Tougher sentences would be applied against those who were convicted a second time and against any person whose offense resulted in bodily injury.

"This legislation is a major victory for women and for women's rights," proclaimed Senator Edward M. Kennedy, a Massachusetts Democrat. "For the first time, Congress has passed a law to protect a woman's constitutional right to choose."[5]

Some right-to-life advocates were outraged by the severity of the new law and denounced it as an unconstitutional attempt to outlaw demonstrations against abortion. "What this bill does is aim the full force of the federal criminal system against a class of Americans who feel passionately about one of the key moral questions of our time," said Senator Don Nickles, an Oklahoma Republican.[6]

In an attempt to prevent antiabortion protesters from blocking access to an abortion clinic and threatening its patients and staff, a judge in 1993 created a "protest-free" zone around an abortion clinic in Melbourne, Florida. This buffer zone extended about 36 feet around the clinic, and police were told to arrest any protesters who picketed, shouted, or chanted in this area. The court order also banned protesters from holding up pictures of aborted fetuses and from trying to speak with any patient or staff member within 300 feet of the clinic.

Right-to-life groups challenged this court order in a lawsuit. They claimed it violated their First Amendment rights of freedom of speech and assembly.

Voting 6 to 3 in 1994, the Supreme Court ruled that the "protest-free" zone around the abortion clinic was constitutional. Expressing the majority opinion, Chief Justice Rehnquist said that this buffer zone curtails "no more speech than necessary to accomplish the governmental interest at stake," which is to protect the patients' right to freely enter the clinic. At the same time, the Court ruled that barring protesters from holding up pictures of aborted fetuses and preventing them from speaking with any patient or staff member within 300 feet of the clinic were unnecessary restrictions on free speech and thus unconstitutional.

Pro-choice advocates praised the Court decision. It "clearly establishes that the right to protest does not include the right to terrorize," said Elaine Metlin of the National Abortion Federation.[7] An opposing opinion was expressed by Clarke Forsythe of Americans United for Life, who said the decision was "an unprecedented restriction on free speech," indicating that "the abortion culture has won out over the First Amendment."[8]

CHAPTER SIX

SEX DISCRIMINATION

In 1873, Supreme Court Justice Joseph P. Bradley, in a case denying women the right to practice law, said that "the natural and proper timidity and delicacy which belongs to the female sex evidently unfits it for many of the occupations of civil life. This is the law of the Creator."[1] Bradley was speaking not only for the Court but also for most Americans, who at that time regarded men as the breadwinners, voters, and lawmakers; women were looked upon as dependent housewives whose chief duties were obeying their husbands and staying home to rear children. This belief that women were intended to be the "weaker" sex—second-class citizens unfit for many occupations and also for most civic duties and legal responsibilities—stood for nearly two centuries as a towering barrier against permitting women to have equal rights and responsibilities. As recently as 1961, the Supreme Court upheld a law making jury service mandatory for men but optional for women.

The civil rights movement of the 1950s and 1960s spurred a growing national concern about all forms of discrimination, including that based on sex. Congress took a step aimed at reducing the inequity between the sexes when it adopted the Equal Pay Act of 1963. More significant legislation was the Civil

Rights Act of 1964, whose Title VII prohibited employment discrimination on the basis of sex, race, religion, and national origin. Lyndon B. Johnson was president when this landmark bill became law. While President Johnson exerted strong pressure to enforce the act's provisions regarding racial discrimination, his administration "made little effort to enforce the prohibition against sexual discrimination in Title VII of the 1964 Civil Rights Act."[2]

The struggle for women's rights did not become a major issue in the courts until the 1970s. Thus, it bypassed the Warren Court but drew careful attention and strong action from the Burger Court.

LEGACY OF THE BURGER COURT

In the 1971 case of *Reed* v. *Reed*, the Burger Court dealt with its first case involving sex discrimination. The case arose after a child in Idaho had died and Sally and Cecil Reed, his adoptive parents who had separated, each filed a petition to serve as administrator of the child's estate. An Idaho court awarded the appointment to the child's father because a state law gave preference to males as estate administrators. Sally Reed contested the law as a violation of the equal protection clause of the Fourteenth Amendment.

For the first time in its history, the Supreme Court declared a law unconstitutional because it discriminated against women. Sex classifications, decreed a unanimous Court, were "subject to scrutiny." Expressing the Court's opinion, Chief Justice Burger declared, "To give a mandatory preference to members of either sex over members of the other . . . is forbidden by the equal protection clause."

Two years later, in *Frontiero* v. *Richardson*, the Supreme Court struck down a federal law that granted male members of the armed forces larger benefits for their families than female members. The Court in 1975 declared unconstitutional that part of the Social Security Act which provided survivor's benefits to widows with small children but not to widowers with small children. In the same year, the Court overturned a Louisiana law that permitted the automatic exemption of women from juries.

The Supreme Court in a 1976 case set down guidelines for determining when classification by gender (sex) is constitutional and when it is not. Oklahoma had a law prohibiting the sale of 3.2 percent beer to males under twenty-one years of age but permitting females eighteen years or older to purchase it. The purpose of the law was to reduce drunk driving, but while it prevented young men from buying beer, it did not prevent them from drinking or possessing it.

The justices voted 7 to 2 to strike down the Oklahoma law. Writing for the majority, Justice Brennan, explained that a classification based on gender is not valid unless it is substantially related to the achievement of an important governmental objective. The Court concluded that even though Oklahoma's effort to promote traffic safety was an important goal, prohibiting the sale but not the possession of beer to males under age twenty-one did not substantially help the state reach that goal.

The Burger Court did not overturn all laws that were gender-based. It upheld the limitation of draft registration to males, and it did not strike down rape laws that punished underage males but not females. While the Court in 1974 required employers to be flexible in granting maternity leaves to pregnant workers, six months later it approved a law excluding pregnancy and childbirth from a state's disability insurance system. The Court also upheld a Florida property tax exemption law that discriminated between widows and widowers.

"The final months of the Burger Court," wrote law professor Wendy W. Williams, "produced a decision involving women and sexuality unique both in the degree of consensus [agreement] reached by the justices and in its commitment to gender equality."[3] The ruling in this case, *Meritor Savings Bank* v. *Vinson* (1986), was based on Title VII of the Civil Rights Act of 1964 rather than on the Constitution. The justices voted unanimously that Title VII prohibited sexual harassment in the workplace because it was a form of sex discrimination. Speaking for the Court, Justice William H. Rehnquist declared that sexual harassment is illegal not only when it results in the loss of a job or a promotion, but also when it creates an offensive or hostile working environment.

THE REHNQUIST COURT

In 1987, the Rehnquist Court decided three major cases involving women's rights. One case dealt with the question of whether women could join organizations whose membership previously had been restricted to men. In Duarte, California, the local Rotary Club had admitted women to what had been an all-male organization. Rotary International then expelled the Duarte chapter and filed a lawsuit charging that it had the right to exclude women.

A California law prohibits discrimination based on sex, and on these grounds the state appeals court upheld the Duarte chapter's policy of accepting women members. Lawyers for Rotary International, however, took the case to the Supreme Court, arguing that California's antidiscrimination law is unconstitutional because it violates members' First Amendment guarantee to associate with whom they please. The Court had to decide between two important rights—freedom of association and equal opportunity for women as well as men.

By a unanimous vote, the Court upheld the right of women to join the Rotary Club. Speaking for all the justices, Powell said that Rotary International "failed to demonstrate that admitting women" would weaken the organization's ability to meet its goals. He added that even if the California law "does work some slight infringement [violation] on Rotary members' right of . . . association, that infringement is justified because it serves the state's compelling interest in eliminating discrimination against women."

The second 1987 case concerning women's rights involved a woman who tried to join an all-male workforce in Santa Clara County in California. The county's transportation agency had developed in 1978 an affirmative action plan calling for a workforce that reflected the ethnic and sexual makeup of the entire workforce in the area that it served. This meant that women should hold more than a third of the jobs in each of the agency's departments. Actually, however, they held very few of the highly skilled jobs. When a position as a road dispatcher became available, Diana Joyce, who had worked nearly ten years at the agency, applied for it. The applicants were tested and interviewed, and Joyce

Ruth Bader Ginsburg (left) and Sandra Day O'Connor (right)
were the first women to be Supreme Court justices. In the 1970s,
Ginsburg acquired a national reputation as an outstanding attorney
in the field of sex discrimination lawsuits.

finished fourth in the competition, a few points lower than the score attained by the highest-scoring man, Paul Johnson. In accord with its affirmative action plan, the agency gave the job to Joyce. Johnson then sued, claiming that he had been the victim of sex discrimination, in violation of Title VII of the 1964 Civil Rights Act.

The Rehnquist Court voted 6 to 3 in favor of Joyce. Delivering the majority opinion, Justice Brennan said that the transportation agency's affirmative action plan had not violated Title VII in giving the job to a qualified woman. Justice Scalia, who dissented along with Chief Justice Rehnquist and Justice White, disagreed sharply. "The Civil Rights Act," declared Scalia, "clearly forbids discrimination; it does not give each . . . racial and sexual group a governmentally determined 'proper' proportion of each job category."

In another 1987 case, the Supreme Court dealt with a situation in which a federal law seemed to conflict with a state law. Congress had passed a law in 1978 stating that in order to prohibit discrimination "on the basis of pregnancy, childbirth, or related medical conditions," pregnant women "shall be treated the same [as other disabled workers] for all employment related purposes, including the receipt of benefits." The California state law, however, said that employers must allow pregnant workers an unpaid disability leave, up to four months, so that they need not fear they will lose their jobs during the time that they are not working. When a woman in Los Angeles sought to regain her job at a savings and loan corporation three months after leaving to have a baby, she was told that her job had been given to someone else. She then contacted the California Department of Fair Employment and Housing, which had the responsibility for enforcing the state's pregnancy leave law. Later, the corporation reinstated her to the same position she had previously held, but decided to file suit in a federal court against the state law.

By a vote of 6 to 3, the Supreme Court upheld the California statute. Writing for the majority, Justice Marshall said that the 1978 federal law was not intended to prohibit states from requiring more benefits for workers disabled by pregnancy than for other temporarily disabled workers. In dissent, Justice Byron R. White declared that the federal law did not give states the right to make laws that gave pregnant women preferred treatment.

Another case pertaining to pregnancy was decided by the Supreme Court in 1991. In this case, women were demanding the right to continue working while they were pregnant, even though their type of job could possibly affect the health of their fetuses. These women were employed by Johnson Controls, a company that made batteries. Lead is used in the production of batteries, and the workers at battery plants can be exposed to lead in the air. High lead levels in the blood may cause unplanned abortions or genetic defects in children, but the degree of risk to pregnant women exposed to lead is uncertain.

Johnson Controls in 1982 adopted a policy prohibiting women who were pregnant or capable of bearing children from holding jobs that could expose them to lead. Two years later, a group of women, represented by their union, challenged this policy in court, claiming that it violated federal laws banning discrimination based on gender or pregnancy. Both a federal judge and a federal appeals court upheld the company's policy as a reasonable measure for promoting industrial safety.

By a 6 to 3 margin in *Auto Workers Union* v. *Johnson Controls Incorporated*, the Supreme Court struck down the company's so-called "fetal protection" regulation. The majority opinion was written by Justice Blackmun, who said, "Decisions about the welfare of future children must be left to the parents who conceive, bear, support, and raise them rather than the employers who hire those parents." Judges, as well as employers, Blackmun declared, have no right to decide "whether a woman's reproduction role is more important to herself and her family than her economic role." Dissenters opposed to this decision were Chief Justice Rehnquist and Justices White and Kennedy.

The Civil Rights Act of 1991, signed into law by President Bush, made it easier for women and minorities to sue their employers for workplace discrimination. Moreover, it gave victims of sexual harassment the right to sue their employers for damages. Previously victims (either women or men) could win only unpaid wages in court cases. But this new civil rights legislation entitled persons who suffer from sexual harassment the right to seek up to $300,000 in damages from their employers.[4]

When the Supreme Court had heard its first sexual harassment case in 1986, it had unanimously ruled that such harassment is illegal when it creates an offensive or hostile working environment. But the Court had left unanswered questions about what actually constituted a hostile environment. Does the victim's job performance or mental health have to suffer? How many off-color jokes, veiled suggestions regarding sexual acts, or demeaning insults does a woman—or man—have to endure before this behavior is classified as sexual harassment and makes it possible for the victim to sue the offender for damages? The members of the Rehnquist Court had to wrestle with these questions when they heard the case of *Harris* v. *Forklift Systems* in 1993.

Teresa Harris had worked as a sales manager for a Tennessee company that sold and rented forklift trucks. Her employer told her offensive jokes, suggested that she might have secured a big contract by promising to have sex with the customer, called her a derogatory name, and made sexist remarks to her, such as "You're a woman—what do you know?" and "We need a man as the rental manager." Harris asserted that her employer's behavior toward her caused her to cry frequently, experience shortness of breath and insomnia, and drink heavily.

When Harris filed a lawsuit against her employer, a federal magistrate dismissed her charges on the grounds that her harassment did not appear to have harmed her psychological well-being and that a reasonable woman in similar circumstances would not have been affected in her job performance by what had happened to Harris. A panel of three male judges on a U.S. appeals court upheld the magistrate's decision. Then the Supreme Court agreed to hear Harris' appeal and determine whether her treatment in the workplace had violated federal civil rights acts. "The case is of extraordinary importance," said Marcia Greenberger of the National Women's Law Center, "because there are so many ways that employers have tried to raise technicalities and new and complicated legal standards and loopholes to weaken the protection against sexual harassment."[5]

The Rehnquist Court ruled unanimously in favor of Harris.

Federal civil rights laws established a "broad rule of workplace equality," wrote Justice O'Connor, and those laws are broken when women or men are subjected to "intimidation, ridicule and insult" by supervisors or coworkers because of their gender. A complaining victim, the Court ordered, can win damages in a lawuit simply by showing that she or he suffered severe and persistent harassment, regardless of whether it hurt that person's job performance or mental health. O'Connor concluded that judges should decide sexual harassment cases by determining whether a "reasonable person" would have viewed the victim's workplace as a "hostile or abusive environment."

Two cases involving possible sex discrimination by colleges were appealed to the Supreme Court in 1993. Conforming to the Constitution's guarantee of equal protection of the laws, in recent years nearly all public colleges and universities that once were limited to only men or women have been enrolling both sexes. One of the few public institutions of higher learning that continued its men-only policy was Virginia Military Institute (VMI), whose distinguished graduates include Civil War General Thomas (Stonewall) Jackson and World War II General George C. Marshall. VMI officials claimed that the school's rigorous program was suitable only to men. In 1990, however, the Justice Department sued VMI on the grounds that its admission policy violated the Fourteenth Amendment.

A federal district court judge ruled in favor of VMI. But a U.S. appeals court reversed this decision, ordering that if VMI wanted to continue receiving government financial aid, it must admit women to its regular program or create a separate "parallel program" providing women a military-type education. The Supreme Court agreed with the appellate court and let its ruling stand.

The other 1993 sex discrimination education case pertained to Colorado State University, which had dropped its women's softball program in 1992 because of budgetary problems. At that time, women composed 48.2 percent of the undergraduate student enrollment, but 77 percent of the school's spending on intercollegiate athletics went to men's teams. Members of the softball team sued, charging the school with violating the 1972 law known as Title IX, which bans sex discrimination in education.

A district court judge decreed that athletic funding for women's sports at Colorado State was not "substantially proportionate to female enrollment" and that dropping the softball team was illegal. The Supreme Court, without comment, let stand this ruling that the university had violated an antibias law.

In 1994, the Supreme Court was asked to decide whether the Civil Rights Act of 1991 could be applied to lawsuits in which employees had been subjected to sexual harassment or racial discrimination before the new law went into effect. If the High Court ruled in their favor, victims of workplace discrimination before the 1991 law was enacted could seek payment of up to $300,000 in damages from their employers. The Rehnquist Court, however, by a 8 to 1 vote, declared that the provisions of the 1991 Civil Rights Act did not apply to verdicts against employers for past discrimination .

Sex bias in the selection of jurors was the subject of another 1994 Supreme Court decision. Traditionally, trial lawyers for the prosecution and defense have been permitted to exclude a specific number of potential jurors (usually six to twelve) without giving a reason. In a paternity suit against James E. Bowman, an Alabama man, the prosecutor moved to exclude all men from the roster of potential jurors. A blood test indicated with 99.9 percent certainty that Bowman was the father of the child born in 1989, and the jury agreed that he had fathered the child. The judge then ordered him to pay child support to the mother.

Bowman appealed that he had not received a fair trial because the prosecutor had insisted that the jury be composed entirely of women. The Alabama Supreme Court upheld the verdict and declared that Bowman had not been the victim of sex discrimination.

The U.S. Supreme Court, by a vote of 6 to 3, overturned the decisions of the lower courts and ruled that Bowman had suffered prejudice because of the all-woman jury selection in his trial. Expressing the opinion of the majority, Justice Blackmun explained that neither women nor men can be excluded from juries because of their gender. "Equal opportunity to participate in the fair administration of justice is fundamental to our democratic system," he said. Besides Blackmun, voting with the majority

were Justices Stevens, Kennedy, O'Connor, Souter, and
Ginsburg. Dissenters were Chief Justice Rehnquist and Justices
Scalia and Thomas.

Even though this Court decision struck down an all-female
jury, it was women who profited the most from its implications.
This was because of the long-standing prejudice in many states
against women's serving on juries. As recently as 1947, sixteen
states continued to exclude women from juries. The 1994
Supreme Court ruling was hailed by a spokeswoman for the
National Women's Law Center as a "landmark decision for
women's rights" that recognizes "the shared history of discrimination faced by women and racial minorities in this country."[6]

CHAPTER SEVEN

RIGHTS OF
THE ACCUSED

Besides safeguarding important freedoms, the Bill of Rights and the Fourteenth Amendment protect the rights of persons accused of crimes. The Fourth Amendment makes unreasonable searches and seizures illegal. The Fifth Amendment prohibits double jeopardy (being tried twice for the same crime) and permits arrested persons to remain silent and not testify against themselves in trials. The Fifth Amendment also forbids the federal government to deprive any person of life, liberty, or property without due process of law; the Fourteenth Amendment applies this same principle to state governments.

The Sixth Amendment states the basic requirements of due process in federal criminal trials. It provides the accused a speedy and public trial, an impartial jury, the right to confront witnesses for the prosecution and to obtain witnesses for the defense, and the right to the assistance of a counsel (a lawyer). The Seventh Amendment guarantees the right to trial by jury, and the Eighth Amendment prohibits cruel or unusual punishment and forbids excessive bail or fines.

Some of the rights of the accused will be discussed in this chapter. Others are discussed in chapters 8 and 9.

LEGACY OF THE WARREN COURT

In a 1938 case, the Supreme Court ordered that defendants in all federal criminal cases be provided a lawyer if they were too poor to pay for legal services. Poor defendants in state cases, however, did not have access to government-paid attorneys except in cases punishable by death or when unusual circumstances—such as illiteracy or mental illness—necessitated the aid of counsel.

In 1963, the Warren Court considered, in *Gideon* v. *Wainwright*, whether to expand the right to counsel. Clarence Earl Gideon had been arrested by Florida police for breaking into a poolroom and robbing money from a jukebox and cigarette machine. When he explained that he could not afford an attorney and asked for one paid by the state, the judge denied his request. Sentenced to five years in prison, Gideon prepared his own petitions, asking higher courts to overturn his conviction because he had been refused his constitutional right to counsel.

When his case reached the Supreme Court, a distinguished Washington attorney, Abe Fortas (later a Supreme Court justice), was appointed to represent Gideon. The Warren Court unanimously voted to reverse Gideon's conviction. Writing for the Court, Justice Black asserted that the Sixth Amendment's right-to-counsel provision was "fundamental and essential to a fair trial" in state as well as in federal courts.

Today, government-paid lawyers, known as public defenders, are the counsels for about eight in ten defendants in criminal cases. But impoverished suspects often are not adequately represented because public defenders, especially in large cities, are confronted with more cases than they should handle. With 13 million criminal charges filed every year, many public defenders must juggle dozens of cases at one time.[1]

In the case of *Escobedo* v. *Illinois* (1964), the Supreme Court linked the right to counsel to the defendant's right to remain silent, which is protected by the Fifth Amendment. Danny Escobedo had been arrested for murder in Illinois. During his police interrogation, he repeatedly asked for the aid of a lawyer, but his request was turned down. Moreover, he was not told that he had the right to remain silent and not answer any questions that

the police asked him. In his trial, statements he had made during
the police interrogation were used against him, and he was convicted. Escobedo appealed the verdict, arguing that because his
right to counsel and his right to remain silent had been violated,
his trial had not been fair and impartial.

The Warren Court voted 5 to 4 in favor of Escobedo.
Expressing the majority opinion, Justice Arthur J. Goldberg
wrote:

> We have . . . learned . . . that no system of criminal justice
> can, or should, survive if it comes to depend for its con-
> tinued effectiveness on the citizens' abdication through
> unawareness of their constitutional rights. No system
> worth preserving should have to *fear* that if an accused is
> permitted to consult with a lawyer, he will become aware
> of, and exercise, these rights. If the exercise of constitu-
> tional rights will thwart the effectiveness of a system of
> law enforcement, then there is something very wrong
> with that system.

Justice White, one of the four dissenters, asserted that the
Escobedo decision frustrated "the legitimate and proper function
of honest and purposeful police investigations." He declared
that this decision stood "as an impenetrable barrier to any interrogation once the accused has become a suspect." White
concluded that *Escobedo* made criminal justice more difficult to
obtain.

The most famous and far-reaching criminal-procedure decision handed down by the Warren Court was *Miranda* v. *Arizona*
(1966). Ernesto Miranda was tried for the kidnapping and rape
of an eighteen-year-old woman in Arizona. He was questioned by
the police for two hours, and then he signed a confession. Before
they interrogated him, the police had failed to advise him of his
right to remain silent and his right to counsel. Statements
Miranda made and the confession he signed during the police interrogation were used against him at his trial. He was convicted
and sentenced to prison for twenty to thirty years. From prison,
Miranda challenged the guilty verdict, declaring that the evidence

used against him had been illegally obtained because it violated his Fifth Amendment protection against self-incrimination and his Sixth Amendment right to counsel.

By a vote of 5 to 4, the Supreme Court reversed Miranda's conviction. Expressing the majority opinion, Chief Justice Warren said that this case raised "questions which go to the roots of our concepts of American criminal jurisprudence." These questions, he continued, involved the restrictions "society must observe consistent with the federal Constitution in prosecuting individuals for crime."

To safeguard the rights of the accused, the Court laid down these special rules: before being questioned suspects have to be informed of their right to remain silent; they have to be told that anything they say can be used against them in court; during police interrogations they have the right to be aided by an attorney, and if they cannot afford an attorney one will be appointed at government expense prior to questioning. A statement obtained without following these rules cannot be used as evidence in a trial, the Court decreed.

The four justices who opposed the *Miranda* decision believed that the Court-established rules handicapped law enforcement officers in carrying out their duty to protect society. Justice Harlan accused the Court of "taking a real risk with society's welfare in imposing its new rules" for police procedures in dealing with suspects. "The social costs of crime are too great to call the new rules anything but a hazardous experimentation," he concluded.

The *Miranda* decision set off a heated controversy throughout the United States, and the argument about its rules still continues. Those who applauded the decision generally agreed with historian John Morton Blum, who said it protected "the rights of all Americans from violation by ignorant and overzealous police. In so doing," Blum continued, "the Court was ruling against the kind of dangerous police procedures that characterized totalitarian governments, fascist and Communist alike."[2]

Opponents of the *Miranda* decision included many members of Congress. Senator John L. McClellan of Arkansas angrily declared, "This 5-4 decision is of such adverse significance to law

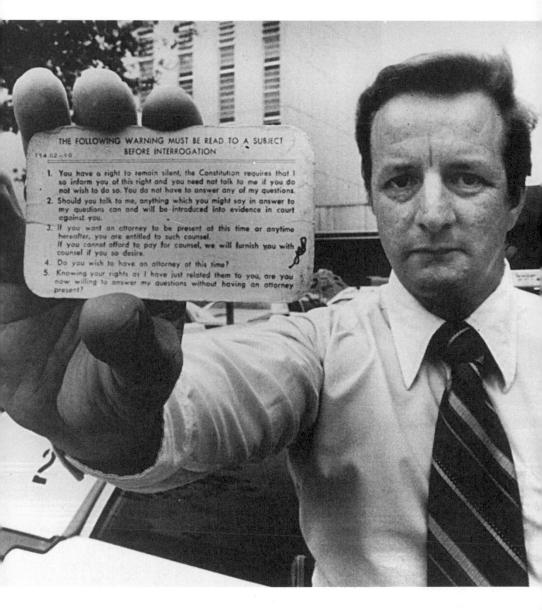

As a result of the 1966 *Miranda* v. *Arizona* ruling, police officers must read suspects their rights when making an arrest, so as not to violate the Fifth and Sixth amendments, which protect the accused from self-incrimination and guarantee their right to counsel.

enforcement that it . . . demands . . . legislation . . . to alleviate the damage it will do to society."[3]

In 1968, Congress approved the Omnibus Crime Control and Safe Streets Act. Included in this act was a provision specifically designed to moderate the effect of the *Miranda* rules. It said that confessions can be used as evidence in federal trials whenever the judge rules that they are voluntary.

LEGACY OF THE BURGER COURT

The Burger Court, more conservative than the Warren Court, rendered some decisions that restricted the *Miranda* rules. In *Harris* v. *New York* in 1971, the Court decided that there could be exceptions to the *Miranda* precedent. The case involved a defendant whose statements in his trial contradicted statements he had made to the police before he was told of his rights.

By a vote of 5 to 4, the Burger Court decreed that voluntary statements made by a defendant not told of his or her rights may still be used to question the suspect's truthfulness if, on the witness stand, that person contradicts earlier statements. Chief Justice Burger, writing for the majority, declared, "It does not follow from *Miranda* that evidence inadmissible [not allowable] against an accused . . . is barred for all purposes," providing there is definite proof that the defendant is lying.

The Court declared in a 1974 case that a statement made by a defendant who had not been advised of his *Miranda* rights could be used to locate a witness for the prosecution. The following year, the Court heard the case of a suspect who had been given the proper *Miranda* warnings, but was told that he would not be able to talk to his lawyer until he reached the police station. In spite of the warnings against self-incrimination, the suspect made incriminating statements on the way to the police headquarters, and these statements were used against him in his trial. The Supreme Court upheld the use of these early statements as evidence and said that they did not violate the *Miranda* rules.

The Burger Court had to determine in 1984 whether police must first advise suspects of their constitutional rights in situations in which public safety is at stake. Benjamin Quarles was chased into a New York City store by police who suspected him of committing a crime. While frisking him, officers noticed an empty shoulder holster and asked where the weapon was. "The gun is over there," replied the suspect, pointing to a nearby carton. After picking up the gun, an officer read Quarles his *Miranda* rights.

The lower courts ruled that both the gun and Quarles's statement about it could not be used as evidence against him because police had not read him his rights beforehand. In a 5 to 4 decision, the Burger Court upheld Quarles's conviction, reasoning that as long as the gun was concealed, people nearby were in danger because it could have been used by an accomplice. Justice Rehnquist, speaking for the majority, said, "We conclude that the need for answers to questions in a situation posing a threat to the public safety outweighs the need for the . . . rule protecting the Fifth Amendment's privilege against self-incrimination."

Justices Stevens, O'Connor, Brennan, and Marshall voted against the Court majority in this case. In dissent, Marshall opposed the public safety exception to *Miranda*, claiming that it "destroys forever the clarity of *Miranda* for both law enforcement officers and members of the judiciary."

In a 1986 case, the justices, voting 6 to 3, ordered that a criminal confession is valid even after police mislead a suspect about an upcoming interrogation and fail to inform him that an attorney wants to see him before he is questioned. The Court majority maintained that there is no need to overturn a conviction when police officers "are less than forthright" regarding an attorney's wish to confer with the suspect. Justice O'Connor, writing the majority opinion, said that a requirement that police officers tell a suspect of an attorney's effort to see him would provide only slight constitutional protection and would come as "a substantial cost to society's legitimate and substantial interest in securing admissions of guilt." In a vigorous dissent, Justice Stevens charged that the Court majority had "flouted the spirit" of the justice system and approved "police deception of the shabbiest kind."

THE REHNQUIST COURT
The Supreme Court decided two 1990 cases that pertained to the provision in the Sixth Amendment which says that "in all crimi-

nal prosecutions, the accused shall enjoy the right . . . to be confronted with the witnesses against him." Before 1990, this part of the Sixth Amendment had been interpreted to mean that the defendant had the right to confront prosecution witnesses face-to-face in the courtroom. However, a Maryland case raised the question of whether child witnesses could, in some situations, testify via closed-circuit TV. Sandra Ann Craig, a preschool teacher in Maryland, had been accused of abusing several children at her nursery. Under a Maryland law, these children had been permitted to testify via closed-circuit television because they feared Craig and because prosecution attorneys said that seeing her in person might have affected the children's testimony. Craig was found guilty, but the Maryland appeals court reversed her conviction, asserting that the defendant's Sixth Amendment rights had been violated.

In a 5 to 4 decision, the Rehnquist Court overturned the Maryland court's ruling and upheld Craig's conviction. Writing the majority opinion, Justice O'Connor pointed out that the jurors were able to hear the children's responses when they were cross-examined by a defense lawyer and that this was a reasonable substitute for confronting the young witnesses in the courtroom. The Sixth Amendment, Justice O'Connor argued, does not "guarantee criminal defendants the absolute right to a face-to-face meeting with the witnesses against them at trial."

The other 1990 case involved an Idaho woman who had been convicted of abusing her child. At her trial, a pediatrician took the witness stand and testified on what he said the woman's two-year-old daughter told him in an office visit. However, the doctor did not tape-record or take careful notes of the child's remarks, and the mother's attorney claimed that the doctor's undocumented testimony should not be allowed as evidence. Voting 5 to 4, the Supreme Court overturned the woman's conviction; the majority of justices believed that there was not sufficient proof that the pediatrician's statements were accurate and trustworthy.

The Fifth Amendment says that no person "shall be compelled in any criminal case to be a witness against himself." Since 1897, the Supreme Court had ruled that only *voluntary* confessions could be used as evidence in trials. This long-standing

Court precedent was tested in a 1991 case involving Oreste Fulminante, an Arizona man suspected of murdering his eleven-year-old stepdaughter. Police did not have enough evidence to file charges against him, and Fulminante left the state.

Later, Fulminante was arrested for another crime and imprisoned in New York. A very small man, Fulminante was afraid that some of the prison inmates might attack him because of the rumors that he was a child murderer. Anthony Sarivola, another prisoner who was secretly an FBI informant, promised Fulminante protection if he would tell the truth about what had happened to his stepdaughter. Fulminante confessed to Sarivola that he had killed the girl. A few weeks later, Fulminante and Sarivola were released from prison, and the Arizona man repeated his confession to Sarivola's wife, Donna. He was returned to Arizona, stood trial for murder, and was convicted. His lawyer appealed the case to the Arizona Supreme Court, which reversed his conviction on the grounds that Fulminante's first confession was coercive, rather than voluntary, because he had made it at a time when he feared that other prisoners might harm him.

The Rehnquist Court had to decide whether the defendant's first confession was voluntary, or if it was involuntary, whether it constituted only a harmless trial error, since Fulminante later confessed the same crime to Donna Sarivola. The Court voted 5 to 4 against the defendant. Expressing the majority opinion, Chief Justice Rehnquist said that it "is essential to preserve the principle that the central purpose of a criminal trial is to decide the factual question of the defendant's guilt or innocence."

Justice White, one of the dissenters, sharply rebuked the Court's decision. He wrote, "Today, a majority of the Court, without any justification, overrules a vast body of precedent . . . and in so doing dislodges one of the fundamental tenets [principles] of our criminal justice system." White declared that ours is a system "in which the state must establish guilt by evidence independently and freely secured and may not by coercion prove its charges against any accused out of his own mouth."

The Rehnquist Court considered in 1993 a case in which a federal district judge had lengthened the prison term of a con-

An all-white, all-male jury in Sumner, Mississippi, 1955. The
Supreme Court has declared such juries unconstitutional.

victed woman because she had apparently lied in her courtroom testimony. The woman, Sharon Dunnigan, was tried for distributing cocaine, which she denied on the witness stand, even though the prosecution proved that she had sold drugs to a government witness while under police surveillance. The trial judge then invoked a provision of the sentencing guidelines that provides for increasing the sentences of defendants who have "willfully impeded or obstructed the administration of justice" at a trial. A federal appeals court ruled that the trial judge had erred in subjecting the defendant to a longer prison term because of "a disbelieved denial of guilt under oath" and that the threat of added prison time placed "an intolerable burden upon the defendant's right to testify in her own behalf."

The Supreme Court decided unanimously that criminal defendants who take the stand and testify falsely in their own defense may constitutionally be subjected to additional prison time for obstructing justice. Writing for the Court, Justice Kennedy said that "a defendant's right to testify does not include a right to commit perjury." Kennedy explained that a defendant who "perjures herself in an unlawful attempt to avoid responsibility is more threatening to society and less deserving of leniency than a defendant who does not so defy the trial process."

Historically, state courts have accepted the principle that a mentally deranged person cannot be held legally responsible for committing a crime. But the use of insanity as a defense has raised some important questions. Was the defendant truly insane at the time of the crime? Even if legally insane, did the defendant commit the crime purposely and with the knowledge that it was wrong? Questions such as these have led some states in recent years to remove the insanity defense from their criminal codes. One of these states was Montana, and in 1994 the Supreme Court was asked to review the case of a Montana man whose insanity plea had been denied at his trial.

The case involved a forest ranger who, on entering her cabin, found food missing and her television set running. When she saw a man standing outside, she locked the doors and phoned for help. The man broke down the door and used a large metal tool to attack the forest ranger, causing her several injuries. When law enforcement officers arrived, the assailant was standing in the cabin and did not resist arrest.

The defendant's attorneys argued that their client suffered from paranoid schizophrenia and was not legally responsible for what he had done. But the prosecutors claimed that he purposely committed the assault and knew it was wrong. He was convicted, and the Montana Supreme Court agreed with the court's verdict that he was guilty and could be imprisoned for his crime.

When the case reached the Rehnquist Court, the justices refused to consider the defendant's appeal. This meant, in effect, that the High Court upheld the Montana rule that had eliminated insanity as a legal defense.

In 1994, the Supreme Court dealt with the case of a convicted child murderer who was interrogated by police in 1982 before he was given the *Miranda* rules. A young girl in California had disappeared, and her body was found in Pasadena after a man saw a turquoise car stop and the driver toss something large from the car trunk. The murdered girl was last seen talking with an ice cream truck driver.

Police discovered that there were two ice-cream truck drivers who worked in the area where the victim lived. They went to the home of Robert Stansbury, one of the drivers, to see if he could give them any information about the crime, but at that time the other driver was their chief suspect. Stansbury went with the officers to the police station and answered their questions for about thirty minutes. When he mentioned that he had borrowed a friend's turquoise Ford the night before, the questioning suddenly stopped, and the police read Stansbury his *Miranda* rights. He was then arrested, charged with the girl's murder, and found guilty of committing the crime.

Stansbury's attorneys appealed, claiming that the police had violated the *Miranda* rules by not telling him about his rights before they questioned him. The California Supreme Court rejected this claim, asserting that Stansbury was not in custody or suspected of committing the crime until after he mentioned driving the turquoise car.

The Rehnquist Court justices unanimously disagreed with the ruling handed down by the state court. They declared that

Stansbury was in custody when he was taken to the police station and should have been informed of his *Miranda* rights before any questioning began. However, the Court did not reverse Stansbury's conviction. Instead, it ordered the California Supreme Court to restudy the case without considering any trial evidence based on what Stansbury said during the period when questioning him violated his constitutional rights.

CHAPTER EIGHT

PROTECTION AGAINST SEARCH AND SEIZURE

The Fourth Amendment provides "the right of the people to be secure in their persons, houses, papers, and effects against unreasonable searches and seizures." To protect this right, the amendment affirms that no search warrants shall be issued, except "upon probable cause . . . and particularly describing the place to be searched, and the persons or things to be seized."

Before the Revolutionary War, when Americans were ruled by Great Britain, the colonists were unable to protect themselves against unjust searches and seizures. Customs officials, armed with orders called Writs of Assistance, were able to hunt anywhere for goods that might have been smuggled into the colonies. They did not need to get a separate warrant for every building they entered or specify the items they were seeking.

Americans have felt more secure since the Fourth Amendment was added to the Constitution. It does not, however, outlaw all searches and seizures. To provide for the public safety, police and other law enforcement officers must be permitted to gather evidence of a crime and to arrest persons suspected of breaking the law. But the Fourth Amendment guarantees that such searches and seizures must be reasonable. It establishes a balance between the individual's right of privacy and the government's need to obtain evidence of a crime and to arrest persons who may have committed a crime.

In the 1914 case of *Weeks* v. *United States*, the Supreme Court declared that evidence taken as a result of "unreasonable searches and seizures" could not be used to convict defendants in federal court trials. In this decision, a precedent known as the *exclusionary rule* was established: evidence seized illegally must be excluded from a trial in any federal court. Such evidence, the Court decreed, involves "a denial of the constitutional rights of the accused," and to admit it as proof of guilt in a criminal trial would be a violation of the "fundamental law of the land." This 1914 rule against unreasonable search and seizure did not, however, pertain to state or local law enforcement officers; the *Weeks* decision was handed down many years before the Supreme Court decided that the Bill of Rights protects defendants in state cases.

LEGACY OF THE WARREN COURT

Nearly half a century later, in the 1961 landmark case of *Mapp* v. *Ohio*, the Supreme Court finally extended the exclusionary rule to evidence presented in state courts. Acting on a tip that illegal gambling equipment was being hidden in Cleveland, Ohio, by Dollree Mapp, the police forced their way into her home without a warrant. They searched the entire home without finding what they were seeking, but they did discover obscene literature that was illegal under Ohio law. The police seized the literature as evidence, and Mapp was convicted for possessing obscene materials.

When her case was appealed to the Supreme Court, the question before the Court was clear: should the Fourth Amendment's prohibition of unreasonable searches apply to the evidence found in Mapp's home and be excluded from a state court trial because it had been illegally obtained? By a vote of 6 to 3, the Warren Court declared that the evidence must be excluded and overturned Mapp's conviction. Writing the majority opinion, Justice Clark said that the evidence had been "secured by official lawlessness in flagrant abuse" of constitutional rights. The states must be required to exclude illegally obtained evidence from state trials,

Clark explained, because to do otherwise would tend "to destroy the entire system of constitutional restraints on which the liberties of the people rest."

There are some situations in which police do not need a warrant to conduct a search or make an arrest. For example, if an officer sees a crime being committed, he or she obviously cannot wait to obtain a warrant before gathering evidence and apprehending the suspect.

The Warren Court also upheld the police practice of "frisking" suspicious persons to search for weapons. It declared, in *Terry* v. *Ohio* (1968), that such searches were permissible without a search warrant or enough information to constitute probable cause for arrest. Chief Justice Warren explained that "there must be a narrowly drawn authority to permit a reasonable search for weapons for the protection of the police officer, where he has reason to believe that he is dealing with an armed and dangerous individual, regardless of whether he has probable cause to arrest the individual for a crime."

Another aspect of search and seizure pertains to eavesdropping, including the wiretapping of a telephone line. In a 1928 decision, the Supreme Court ruled that listening in on a private conversation without a court warrant did not violate the Fourth Amendment.

This issue surfaced again in *Katz* v. *United States* in 1967. Charles Katz was charged with illegal gambling activities. Most of the evidence used against him came from a listening and recording device attached to the outside of a public telephone booth where Katz had secret conversations.

Reversing the 1928 ruling, the Warren Court, by a vote of 7 to 1, struck down Katz's conviction and decreed that warrantless eavesdropping was prohibited by the Fourth Amendment. Justice Stewart, writing for the majority, declared:

. . . the Fourth Amendment protects people, not places. What a person knowingly exposes to the public, even in his own home or office, is not a subject of Fourth Amendment protection. . . . But what he seeks to preserve as private, even in an area accessible to the public, may be constitutionally protected . . . .

What [Katz] sought to exclude when he entered the booth was not the intruding eye—it was the uninvited ear. He did not shed his right to do so simply because he made his calls from a place where he might be seen.

The year after the *Katz* decision, Congress passed the Crime Control and Safe Streets Act that laid down the rules for legal eavesdropping. A warrant to wiretap or "bug" someone's conversation must be obtained from a judge or a Justice Department official who has been convinced by the police or FBI that there is probable cause of criminal activity which may be detected by the electronic device.

LEGACY OF THE BURGER COURT
The Burger Court continued to define which searches are reasonable and which are not. In 1969, it narrowed the limits of warrantless searches. By a 6 to 2 vote in *Chimel* v. *California*, the Court ruled that when the police legally arrest a person, they must restrict their warrantless search to the immediate area around the suspect from which he or she could obtain a weapon or destroy evidence. A person's entire dwelling cannot be searched simply because he or she is arrested there.

A case that drew national attention in 1978 involved police searching the offices of a university newspaper. Following an unruly demonstration at the Stanford University Hospital, protesters barricaded themselves in the hospital administrative offices. When they refused to leave, police were summoned. Some demonstrators attacked the police with clubs, and nine officers were injured.

The *Stanford Daily,* a student newspaper, published photos of the clash, and from these the police were able to identify two of the attackers. They believed that in the newspaper files there might be negatives of additional photos showing other rioters. The police obtained a warrant to search the paper's offices. The warrant contained no accusation against the newspaper, and the search provided only the photos that the paper had printed.

Claiming that its First and Fourth Amendment rights had been violated, the *Stanford Daily* sued the Palo Alto police, in the name of Police Chief James Zurcher. Attorneys for the newspaper claimed that since no one in the newsrooms was a suspect in the crime, the police should have obtained a court order called a *subpoena* rather than a warrant in seeking the photos. Lawyers for the police argued that to require a subpoena for searches of nonsuspects' property would create a risk that the evidence might be destroyed before the search took place.

The Supreme Court decided, by a vote of 5 to 3, that the use of a search warrant in this case was permissible. Expressing the majority opinion, Justice White declared that " . . . valid warrants may be issued to search *any* property, whether or not occupied by a third party, at which there is probable cause to believe that . . . evidence of a crime will be found."

In dissent, Justice Stevens questioned the possible effects of the Court's decision. "Countless law abiding citizens," he said, ". . . may have documents in their possession that relate to an ongoing criminal investigation. The consequences of subjecting this large category of persons to unannounced police searches are extremely dangerous."

The Burger Court, in 1978, exercised its power to declare unconstitutional part or all of an act passed by Congress. In *Marshall* v. *Barlows, Inc.*, the justices voted 5 to 3 to strike down a provision of the Occupational Safety and Health Act of 1970 that allowed warrantless inspection of businesses. The Court decreed that an Occupational Safety and Health Administration (OSHA) inspector must obtain a search warrant when a business owner objects to a warrantless search, but a warrant can be obtained without the owner's knowledge.

The Supreme Court, in *United States* v. *Leon* (1984), ruled that illegally obtained evidence may be used by the prosecution during a trial if the police who seized it had a search warrant and thought they were acting legally—only to find that because of a technicality their search was actually illegal. This ruling, based on a 6 to 3 vote, was the Court's first exception to the exclusionary rule it had adopted seventy years earlier, barring all use of illegally seized evidence in a federal trial. It was limited to a situation in which police had a warrant and executed a search in accord with it, only to have the warrant later found defective. Delivering the majority opinion, Justice White said that excluding valid evidence because of a technicality "exacts too high a price from society."

Ever since 1925, the Supreme Court had upheld convictions of suspicious persons whose automobiles had been searched by police without warrants. The Court, in 1985, extended warrantless searches to include motor homes. Chief Justice Burger, speaking for the majority, explained that a motor home is more like a car than a dwelling and people expect to have less privacy in a motor home that can travel on the open road.

Besides checking automobiles and motor homes, another way to search for evidence is to use airplanes and helicopters. In 1986, the Burger Court heard a case involving a California man suspected by the police of growing marijuana in his backyard. Instead of obtaining a search warrant to inspect his property, the police chartered a plane and flew over his backyard at an altitude of about 1,000 feet. They noticed the marijuana and then arrested the owner of the property for illegally growing these plants. The defendant claimed that this warrantless aerial surveillance violated his Fourth Amendment protection against unreasonable searches.

Voting 5 to 4, the Supreme Court justices upheld his conviction. Writing for the majority, Chief Justice Burger declared, "In an age where private and commercial flight in the airways is routine, it is unreasonable for [the defendant] to expect that his marijuana plants were constitutionally protected from being observed with the naked eye from an altitude of 1,000 feet."

Justice Powell, one of the dissenters, challenged Burger's comparison of the police air search with what would normally be observed on regularly scheduled commercial flights. He asserted that there is little chance that airplane passengers would be able or willing to spot criminal activities from the sky. "Aerial surveillance," Powell said, "is nearly as intrusive on family privacy as physical trespass. . . . It would appear that, after today, families can expect to be free of official surveillance only when they retreat behind the walls of their home."

THE REHNQUIST COURT

Aerial surveillance was the subject of one of the earliest Rehnquist Court cases. In this instance, a police officer, flying on a helicopter patrol at an altitude of about 400 feet, spotted marijuana growing in a greenhouse in La Mesa, California. A county sheriff then obtained a warrant, confiscated the plant, and arrested a person living on the property.

In this 1987 case, the Supreme Court voted 7 to 2 in favor of the defendant and upheld a state court order asserting that the low-altitude inspection violated the Fourth Amendment. The Court seemed to be saying in its 1986 and 1987 rulings that aerial surveillance is permissible at an altitude of 1,000 feet but not permissible at an altitude of 400 feet. Adding to this confusion, the Court decreed, in *Florida* v. *Riley* (1989), that the police may use low-flying helicopters to search for drugs.

The Rehnquist Court heard several other cases pertaining to searches for drugs. It decisions generally reflected the conservative beliefs of the majority of justices, who tended to favor the need for protecting society more than the defense of individual rights. One 1988 case involved federal narcotics agents who, acting without a warrant, broke down the doors of a warehouse and found marijuana inside. Then they went to a judge and obtained a warrant to search the warehouse and seize the marijuana.

After the drug dealers had been convicted in the lower courts, they appealed to the Supreme Court on the grounds that the federal agents searched their warehouse before they got a warrant. The justices agreed that the first search had been illegal, but, by a 4 to 3 vote, they upheld the drug dealers' convictions. They reasoned that if the agents had seen enough evidence to justify getting a warrant, this evidence should not have been excluded from the trial simply because it was found before the warrant was obtained. Expressing the opinion of the majority, Justice Scalia said, "While the government should not profit from its illegal activity, neither should it be placed in a worse position than it would otherwise have occupied."

The Rehnquist Court's decisions tend to favor the need to protect society more than the defense of individual rights.

Justice Marshall, one of the dissenters, argued that the Court decision "encourages illegal searches." He declared that a dangerous precedent is established when "the police know in advance that they have little to lose and much to gain by forgoing the bother of obtaining a warrant and undertaking an illegal search."

In another 1988 case, the Supreme Court dealt with the question of whether the police, without a warrant, can search garbage left at curbside in front of a person's house. Believing that Billy Greenwood of Laguna Hills, California, was a drug dealer, the police asked the local garbage collector to give them the plastic bags in front of Greenwood's house. Inside the bags officers discovered articles used for dispensing drugs and a little cocaine. The police then obtained a search warrant, entered Greenwood's house, and found several pounds of cocaine and some hashish.

Greenwood claimed that the original warrantless search of his trash bags violated his Fourth Amendment rights. The California Supreme Court had decided in 1971 that searches of discarded trash were unconstitutional, and state courts were obliged to follow that rule.

The Rehnquist Court, however, reversed the decision of the California courts. Voting 6 to 2, the justices decreed that incriminating evidence obtained from garbage without a warrant could be used against the defendant. Delivering the majority opinion, Justice White said the search was valid because Greenwood could have no "reasonable" expectation of privacy in his garbage. "It is common knowledge," White declared, "that plastic garbage bags left on or at the side of a public street are readily accessible to animals, children, scavengers, snoops, and other members of the public. . . . What a person knowingly exposes to the public is not a subject of Fourth Amendment protection."

In dissent, Justice Brennan, expressed an opposing opinion. "A single bag of trash testifies eloquently to the eating, reading, and recreational habits of the person who produced it," he wrote. "Scrutiny of another's trash is contrary to commonly accepted notions of civilized behavior."

The Supreme Court decided in 1989 two cases pertaining to the warrantless testing of certain persons for the use of drugs. One case involved new federal regulations that required drug and alcohol testing of railroad employees after an accident. These regulations were imposed after an incident in which two trains collided, and sixteen persons were killed. The engineer and brakeman on one of the trains were found to have drugs in their bodies. The railroad workers' union challenged the mandatory, warrantless drug testing as an unreasonable search prohibited by the Fourth Amendment.

Voting 7 to 2 in *Skinner* v. *Railway Labor Executives Association*, the Rehnquist Court upheld the Federal Railroad Administration's regulations. Testing individuals for drugs and alcohol constituted searches, the Court admitted, but the majority of justices believed such searches were reasonable in light of the government's compelling interest in protecting public safety, and warrants were not required.[1]

The other 1989 drug testing case was different from the railroad workers' case because it did not apply to persons whose negligent behavior might have already caused serious accidents. In 1986, U.S. Customs commissioner William Von Raab ordered drug testing for customs employees who applied for promotions to positions that required overseeing the prohibition against drug shipments, carrying firearms, or the handling of sensitive information that could be useful to drug dealers. Von Raab did not expect to find large numbers of drug users in the U.S. Customs Service. By the time that the Supreme Court ruled on the constitutionality of the drug tests, they had been given to 3,600 customs employees, only five of whom tested positive for some illegal substance.[2]

Lawyers for the customs workers' union contended that such warrantless tests were violating the privacy of many innocent employees who had given no cause to be suspected of drug use. They also claimed that forcing these persons who sought promotions to undertake urine tests for drug substances was a humiliating, degrading experience.

The Rehnquist Court was closely divided in regard to *National Treasury Employees Union* v. *Von Raab*. By a 5 to 4 vote, the Court upheld the mandatory drug testing required by the Customs Service. There were some surprising switches in the way justices voted. Scalia, usually associated with the Court's other conservative members, deserted their ranks to vote against the majority. On the other hand, liberal-leaning justice Blackmun voted to support the drug testing decision, thus providing the necessary fifth vote for the decision. As expected, the other four votes for the majority position came from conservatives Rehnquist, White, Kennedy, and O'Connor.

Justice Kennedy, writing for the majority, said, "The Government's compelling interests in preventing the promotion of drug users" to key positions "outweighs the privacy interests of those who seek promotion." This type of search, he asserted, is reasonable and may be conducted without a warrant and without any suspicion of an employee.

In dissent, Justice Scalia attacked the Customs Service drug testing rules as an immolation (sacrificial destruction) ". . . of privacy and human dignity in symbolic opposition to drug use. . . . Those who lose," he wrote, " . . . are not just the Customs Service employees, whose dignity is thus offended, but all of us—who suffer a coarsening of our national manners."

Searches for drugs in Mexico provided the basis for a case that the Supreme Court dealt with in 1990. Mexican police, at the request of U.S. marshals, had arrested Rene Verdugo-Urquidez, an alleged smuggler of drugs into the United States. The Mexican authorities handed the suspect over to U.S. marshals at the border crossing near San Diego, California. Then agents of the U.S. Drug Enforcement Administration searched Verdugo Urquidez's two homes in Mexico and seized papers that they believed were records of marijuana shipments.

When the Mexican suspect was tried for drug smuggling in a San Diego federal court, his lawyers contended that their client's records had been illegally seized without a search warrant. Both the trial judge and the Ninth Circuit Court of Appeals agreed that the records belonging to the defendant should be excluded as evidence because their seizure had violated the Fourth Amendment.

The case was appealed to the Supreme Court, which had to decide whether the ban on unreasonable searches extended to foreign countries. By a 6 to 3 vote, the justices decreed that the controversial records could be used as evidence against Verdugo-

Urquidez. Chief Justice Rehnquist, writing for the majority, declared, "The purpose of the Fourth Amendment was to protect the people of the United States against arbitrary action by their own Government. It was never suggested that the provision was intended to restrain the actions of the federal government against aliens outside of the United States territory."

In 1990, the Supreme Court, voting 6 to 3, upheld the police practice of stopping motorists at checkpoints to determine whether they are sober. The following year, by the same 6 to 3 margin, the Rehnquist Court decreed that it was legal for police in Fort Lauderdale, Florida, to board trains and buses at station stopovers and request that passengers let them look through their luggage for drugs. Since passengers retained the right to decline the officers' requests, the Court ruled that such voluntary searches were constitutional.

In *Terry* v. *Ohio* in 1968, the Warren Court had upheld the right of the police to frisk suspicious persons to search for weapons, and the Rehnquist Court dealt with the same subject twenty-five years later. On the evening of November 9, 1989, two police officers in Minneapolis, Minnesota, had noticed Timothy Dickerson leave a house where they thought drugs were being sold. The officers stopped Dickerson and began patting his clothing. They found no weapons but continued to search him and discovered cocaine in one of his pockets. Dickerson was convicted for the possession of an illegal drug, but the Minnesota Supreme Court overturned his conviction on the grounds that the cocaine could not be used as evidence because it was uncovered without a warrant during a search for weapons.

When this case was decided by the Supreme Court in 1993, by a vote of 6 to 3 the justices decreed that the seized cocaine could not be used as evidence against Dickerson. Writing for the majority, Justice White explained that as soon as it is established that the suspect has no weapon, the police may not continue a warrantless search for an incriminating substance that could be concealed in his pockets. However, White added, if the illegal substance is "immediately apparent" before the weapon search is completed, it can be used as evidence against the suspect.

Drugs figured prominently in other 1993 cases decided by

the Rehnquist Court. Congress had enacted a law in 1989 stating that any property that has been used in any manner to help carry out a drug crime is subject to seizure by government officers. Complying with this act and similar laws in most states, government agents have often seized houses, apartment buildings, cars, and boats that belonged to persons involved in drug crimes.

One case that the Court considered in 1993 pertained to a South Dakota man whose mobile home and automobile repair shop had been confiscated after he was found guilty of selling 2 grams of cocaine. The Court ruled unanimously that this punishment was much too harsh for the crime that had been committed and that it violated the Eighth Amendment's protection against "cruel and unusual punishments" and "excessive fines."

The same year, the Rehnquist Court dealt with another drug-crime case involving seizure of property. In 1989, without prior notice, federal agents in Hawaii had seized a house and land belonging to James Good, who previously had served a year in jail after marijuana was discovered in his home. Good filed a lawsuit claiming that his constitutional rights had been violated by government officers who confiscated his property without first notifying him and giving him the opportunity to present his arguments at a court hearing prior to the seizure. Both a district court and a U.S. court of appeals agreed with Good's claim.

By a margin of 5 to 4, the Supreme Court also voted to uphold Good's position. Those who voted in favor of Good were Justices Kennedy, Blackmun, Souter, Stevens, and Ginsburg. Kennedy wrote the majority opinion, saying, "The right to prior notice and a hearing is central to the Constitution's command of due process." Only in "extraordinary situations," he declared, can the government be permitted to confiscate property before giving the owner a proper hearing in which he or she can present reasons why this seizure should not be allowed. Such extraordinary situations could pertain to cars or boats that might be quickly moved and hidden. but not to a house and land.

CHAPTER NINE

CAPITAL PUNISHMENT

T he Constitution says nothing about capital punishment, which is the death penalty for conviction of a serious crime. The Eighth Amendment forbids cruel and unusual punishment, but it does not specify what kinds of punishment fit this definition.

Capital punishment is an issue that has sharply divided the American public. Many people believe that the death penalty is an appropriate punishment for individuals who commit murder or other vicious crimes. They also contend that executions may serve as a warning to potential criminals that they could be sentenced to die for acts that endanger the public safety. Other people believe that capital punishment is a cruel, barbaric practice that might have been acceptable in earlier times but should not be permitted as part of a modern, supposedly humane, system of justice. They question whether the death penalty seriously deters other potential lawbreakers from committing crimes.

LEGACY OF THE WARREN COURT
Capital punishment was not one of the issues that frequently came before the Warren Court. The most important case on this subject was *Witherspoon* v. *Illinois*, decided in 1968. In *Witherspoon,*

the Court concluded that states could not exclude from juries all persons opposed to the death penalty because such juries did not fairly represent the views of the entire community.

Writing for the majority, Justice Stewart said that a jury composed exclusively of those favoring capital punishment "cannot speak for the community. . . . In its quest for a jury capable of imposing the death penalty, the State produced a jury uncommonly willing to condemn a man to die."

LEGACY OF THE BURGER COURT

The Burger Court followed a zigzagging course in its attitude toward capital punishment. In *McGautha* v. *California* in 1971, the Court, by a vote of 6 to 3, upheld a state law that left completely to the discretion (judgment) of the jury the decision to impose the death penalty on a convicted defendant.

The next year, however, the Burger Court did an about-face and reversed its *McGautha* ruling. The Court handed down decisions in three related cases: *Furman* v. *Georgia*, *Branch* v. *Texas*, and *Jackson* v. *Georgia*. By a vote of 5 to 4 in all three cases, the Court struck down all existing death penalty laws on the grounds that they violated the Eighth Amendment and the Fourteenth Amendment. The five justices in the majority had been members of the activist Warren Court: Brennan, Marshall, Douglas, White, and Stewart. The four dissenters were justices appointed by President Nixon: (Chief Justice) Burger, Blackmun, Powell, and Rehnquist.

Nine separate opinions were written on this controversial ruling. Two of the justices in the majority, Brennan and Marshall, felt that standards of decency had evolved to the point where capital punishment no longer could be tolerated under any circumstances. The three other justices in the majority focused on the procedures by which some criminals were selected for the death penalty. As Justice Stewart pointed out, only a few convicted defendants were executed while many others were sent to prison for the same crimes. He asserted that "the Eighth and Fourteenth Amendments cannot tolerate the infliction of a sentence of death under legal systems that permit this unique penalty to be so wantonly [unjustly] and so freakishly imposed."

While executions throughout the United States were stopped in 1972, the Supreme Court left open two procedures states could follow in rewriting their capital punishment laws. One was to make the death sentence mandatory (required) for specific crimes, which would eliminate the "wanton" and "freakish" aspects of laws that let some criminals be executed while others lived. The second procedure called for two stages in trials involving crimes that might be punishable by death. In the first stage, the guilt or innocence of the defendant would be decided. In the second stage, a separate hearing would be held to determine whether the circumstances leading to the crime justified the death penalty.

Most of the states passed new death penalty laws, but the Burger Court decreed that some of them were unconstitutional. In 5 to 4 decisions in 1976, it struck down laws in North Carolina and Louisiana that had made death the required punishment for all defendants convicted of first-degree murder. The Court majority concluded that these state laws showed no consideration for the defendant or for any special circumstances pertaining to the crime.

But on the same day that the Court overturned the mandatory death penalty laws of North Carolina and Louisiana, it approved, by a vote of 7 to 2, the two-stage procedure that had been set up in three other states. In one of these cases, *Gregg* v. *Georgia*, seven justices agreed that "the punishment of death does not invariably [always] violate the Constitution." Expressing the opinion of the majority, Justice Stewart said that the death penalty is "suitable to the most extreme of crimes."

After 1976, the Burger Court usually upheld as constitutional the two-stage procedure in capital punishment laws adopted by many states. On the other hand, it generally struck down state laws making the death penalty mandatory for certain crimes. In 1977, the Court overturned a Georgia law that made

The electric chair has been the form of execution most used in the United States.

rape a crime punishable by death and a Louisiana law that made the death penalty mandatory for a person convicted of the first-degree murder of a police officer. The following year, it struck down Ohio's death penalty law for convicted murderers because it did not allow juries to consider any special circumstances before the sentence was imposed.

THE REHNQUIST COURT

In general, the Rehnquist Court has taken a tough attitude toward defendants appealing the death penalty. In 1987, the Court expanded the grounds for capital punishment, which previously had applied only to actual murderers. By a 5 to 4 vote, it ruled that it is constitutional to execute persons convicted of being accomplices if they played a major role in a crime leading to a murder and displayed reckless indifference to the value of human life.

On the following day, the Rehnquist Court decided a case involving Warren McCleskey, a black man who shot to death a white police officer in Georgia. McCleskey's attorneys claimed that sentencing the defendant to a death penalty was an act of racial discrimination. They referred to a study which showed that in Georgia killers of whites were punished more severely than killers of blacks. In that southern state, the murderer of a white was more than four times more likely to be sentenced to death than a person who murdered a black.[1]

Despite these statistics suggesting racial bias, the Court voted 5 to 4 to uphold Georgia's death penalty system and the execution of McCleskey. "Apparent discrepancies [differences] in sentencing are an inevitable part of our criminal system," explained Justice Powell in the majority opinion. "If we accept McCleskey's claim that racial bias has . . . tainted the capital sentencing decision, we could soon be faced with similar claims as to other types of penalty."

In dissent, Justice Brennan took the position that sentencing McCleskey to death was a continuation of the nation's long history of racial discrimination. "Warren McCleskey's evidence," he wrote, "confronts us with the subtle and persistent influence of the past. . . . We ignore him at our peril, for we remain imprisoned by the past as long as we deny its influence in the present."

The Rehnquist Court did not always take the side of the prosecution in capital punishment cases. In *Booth* v. *Maryland* (1987), the Court, again by a 5 to 4 vote, decreed that a jury considering the fate of an alleged murderer may not be told about the impact of the crime on the victim's family. The majority of justices agreed that the emotional statements made by the victim's grieving relatives could prevent the defendant from receiving a fair trial.

In 1989, the Rehnquist Court handed down three major decisions that further extended the grounds for capital punishment. All three of these rulings were based on a close 5 to 4 vote. In each case, the justices in the majority included the three appointed by President Reagan: O'Connor, Scalia, and Kennedy, along with Chief Justice Rehnquist and Justice White. The four dissenting justices were Brennan, Marshall, Blackmun, and Stevens.

Two of the cases involved convicted murderers who were sixteen and seventeen years old. The Court decided that these minors had received a fair trial and it was not a cruel or unusual punishment to give them death sentences.

Justice Scalia, writing the opinion of the majority in the case of the sixteen-year-old defendant, said that "our job is to identify the evolving standards of decency . . . to determine not what they should be but what they are." He pointed out that of the thirty-seven states that then permitted capital punishment, only twelve prohibited a death sentence for persons under eighteen, and three others forbade it for those under seventeen. "This does not establish the degree of national consensus [agreement] to label a particular punishment cruel and unusual," Scalia concluded.

In an angry dissent, Justice Brennan wrote, "We have never insisted that a punishment [be] rejected unanimously by the States before we may judge it cruel and unusual."

In the other major 1989 case, the Court ruled that a mentally retarded murderer could be put to death. The majority of justices maintained that the constitutional ban on cruel and unusual punishment does not deny a state the power to execute a mentally retarded person who was found competent to be tried in court, whose defense of legal insanity was rejected, and who was properly convicted.

Writing the majority opinion, Justice O'Connor contended that there is no bar to the execution of retarded criminals so long as juries are permitted to consider mental retardation as one factor in deciding on a death sentence. "While a national consensus against execution of the mentally retarded may someday emerge," she said, "there is insufficient evidence of such a consensus today."

Some criminal-law experts were concerned about the message sent out by the Supreme Court's 1989 death penalty decisions. Henry Schwarzchild, director of the American Civil Liberties Union's Capital Punishment Project, claimed that when the Court "merely reacts to the wishes of the general society," it gives up "its responsibility to make constitutional judgments."[2] Harvard law professor Alan Dershowitz declared, "By executing the retarded and people who aren't old enough to vote or serve in the Army, we're doing something barbarous."[3]

In the 1990s, under Chief Justice Rehnquist's leadership, the Supreme Court has handed down a series of rulings that severely restrict prisoners on Death Row from reopening their cases through a writ of *habeas corpus,* which allows federal judges to hear a state prisoner's claim that he or she is being held in violation of the Constitution. (Habeas corpus, guaranteed in the Constitution, is a court order directing an official who has a person in custody to bring that individual to court and to show cause for his or her detention. It may be used by convicted persons to reopen their cases on the ground of illegal detention because of rights denied before or during their trials.) Rehnquist and the other conservative justices on the Supreme Court have asserted that habeas corpus claims clog the federal courts with seemingly endless appeals, cause disrespect for the decisions made by state courts, and delay just punishment for the condemned.

In a 1991 ruling, the High Court upheld the death sentence of convicted murderer Roger Coleman, whose lawyer had bungled his client's case by filing a court appeal one day after the allotted time limit had expired. Coleman maintained that he was innocent, and his lawyer claimed to have newly discovered evidence that cast doubt on whether Coleman committed the crime. But the Supreme Court, by a 6 to 3 vote, decreed that a "procedural default"—filing a valid claim one day late—bars a defendant from appealing to a federal court.

A somewhat similar case was decided in 1993. Leonel Herrera, a Texas drug runner, was convicted and sentenced to die for the murder of two police officers in 1982. Shortly before the 1992 date scheduled for Herrera's execution, his lawyers found new evidence that they said proved his innocence. Witnesses came forward to say that the condemned man's brother, Raul, who died in 1984, actually committed the murders. One witness was Raul's son, who said he saw his father shoot the officers. Another witness, a former judge and friend of Raul's, said that Raul told him that he—not Leonel—had been the killer.

The Texas state prosecutors, however, refused to believe this new evidence was true; it had been revealed many years after the crime occurred and implicated a dead man who could not dispute the claim. When the state courts refused to reopen Herrera's case, his lawyers filed a habeas corpus petition in a federal court. They contended that the Constitution's ban on cruel and unusual punishment would be violated by the execution of someone who is "actually innocent" of the crime.

When *Herrera* v. *Texas* finally was decided by the Supreme Court—more than a decade after the crime had been committed—six justices voted to uphold the death sentence. Chief Justice Rehnquist, speaking for the majority, declared that juries are given the power to determine the guilt or innocence of a defendant. After a person is convicted of murder, "the presumption of innocence disappears," he said, and federal judges have no power to interfere with the jury's verdict. Rehnquist maintained that federal courts "should intervene only when state courts violate constitutional procedures" and not "to correct errors of fact." He conceded, however, that in a "truly extraordinary" case in which new evidence conclusively shows that a convicted defendant is definitely innocent, a federal judge can block an execution.

In dissent, Justice Blackmun argued that strong claims of innocence must be considered, even if they are filed long after the date of the crime. "The execution of a person who can show that he is innocent comes perilously close to simple murder," Blackmun concluded.

"I am an innocent man and something very wrong is taking place tonight."[4] Leonel Herrera said this shortly before he died in May 1993 by lethal injection at Texas's Huntsville prison.

In 1994, Justice Blackmun received widespread attention for a minority opinion he wrote. He was the lone dissenter in a case in which the other eight justices voted to allow the execution of a convicted murderer to proceed. "From this time forward," Blackmun announced, "I shall no longer tinker with the machinery of death. I believe that the death penalty, as currently administered, is unconstitutional." The problem, he said, is that we have a system ". . . that we know must wrongly kill some defendants, a system that fails to deliver the fair, consistent, and reliable sentences of death required by the Constitution." Blackmun then expressed sympathy for the accused man who was facing a lethal injection.

Justice Scalia replied to Blackmun's concern about the man who was to be executed. He declared that much greater concern should be felt for the victim of the crime, who was "ripped by a bullet suddenly and unexpectedly, with no opportunity to prepare himself or his affairs and left to bleed to death on the floor of a tavern. The death-by-injection which Justice Blackmun describes," Scalia said, "looks pretty desirable next to that."

The Supreme Court in recent years has seldom overturned a death sentence, but a 1994 case provided an exception to this tradition. Jonathan D. Simmons, a South Carolina man, had been found guilty of two sexual assaults before being convicted for the murder of a woman. A South Carolina law decrees that a person found guilty of three crimes such as Simmons committed would be imprisoned for life without parole if the death sentence was not imposed. But neither the judge nor the prosecutors in the Simmons case explained this to the jury. So the jurors, possibly believing that Simmons would eventually be freed from prison if they did not give him the death penalty, sentenced him to die.

By a vote of 7 to 2, the Supreme Court struck down the defendant's death sentence because the jurors had not been told that under no circumstances would Simmons be set free. Writing the majority opinion, Justice Blackmun said that the state's "refusal to provide the jury with accurate information" violated the defendant's constitutional guarantee of due process of law.

On the last day of its session ending in June 1994, the Rehnquist Court handed down two decisions in capital punishment cases. By a 5 to 4 vote, the Court ruled that federal district judges can postpone executions of convicts who have exhausted their state appeals to give them a chance to get lawyers who will file a habeas corpus appeal in a federal court. The case involved a poor defendant who argued that without the postponement of his execution, he would die before he could find a lawyer to prepare a habeas corpus petition without charging for this service. Expressing the opinion of the majority, Justice Blackmun declared that federal law requires the government to supply a lawyer for poor defendants seeking a habeas corpus review and that federal judges have the power to postpone executions so that lawyers can prepare the appeals.

In the other capital punishment case, the Court voted 8 to 1 to uphold the California death penalty law. This law had been challenged on the grounds that instructions to jurors are too vague and that jurors are told to take into account a variety of factors when deciding the defendant's punishment. Speaking for the majority, Justice Kennedy said that jury instructions are constitutional when they have "some commonsense core of meaning that criminal juries should be capable of understanding."

CHAPTER TEN

HOW MUCH HAS THE SUPREME COURT CHANGED?

This chapter summarizes major Supreme Court decisions discussed in previous chapters. Also, it helps answer these questions: To what extent have the philosophy and the rulings of the Court changed in the past four decades? To what extent have the precedents set by the Warren Court and the Burger Court been followed by the Rehnquist Court? How have important Court decisions affected the lives of Americans?

THE ESTABLISHMENT OF RELIGION

The Warren Court interpreted the First Amendment clause forbidding laws "respecting an establishment of religion" as a command to observe a strict separation of church and state. In 1962, the justices voted to prohibit the recitation of a nondenominational prayer in any public school; the following year they decreed that reading the Bible as a devotional exercise in public schools also violated the First Amendment. When an Arkansas law forbidding the classroom teaching of evolution was considered by the Warren Court in 1968, it was struck down as unconstitutional.

The Burger Court had to decide whether all government aid to religious and other private schools was contrary to the First

Amendment. In *Lemon* v. *Kurtzman* (1971), the Court overturned state laws that permitted such practices as using public funds to pay the salaries of private school teachers and to buy textbooks and instructional materials for private schools. This ruling, however, did not shut off entirely every form of government aid to religious and other private schools. The Court said that for such aid to be constitutional, it must have a nonreligious purpose, it must neither promote nor undermine religion, and it must not cause the government to become excessively entangled with religion.

A case involving the display of a Christian crèche in a Christmas display on government-owned property produced a sharply divided Court decision in 1984. The chief issue was whether the Nativity scene was primarily a religious symbol or a cultural exhibit expressing the widely approved ideals of peace and goodwill. Voting 5 to 4, the Court upheld its constitutionality.

In 1985, the school prayer controversy was renewed, but this time its supporters called for a moment of silence rather than a spoken prayer. The Burger Court, following the Warren Court precedent, declared that the school-imposed moment of silence was similar to a prayer and defied the First Amendment.

The Rehnquist Court in 1987 considered a case arising from a Louisiana law requiring public school science teachers who taught about evolution to give equal time to teaching the "creation-science" theory. This theory contends that God created humans in the manner described in the Bible. The justices voted 7 to 2 to strike down this law, with the Court's two most conservative members, William H. Rehnquist and Antonin Scalia, dissenting.

In 1989, the Court had to determine the constitutionality of a Pittsburgh holiday exhibit that included both a Christian crèche and a Jewish menorah next to a Christmas tree at the city hall and county courthouse. The justices voted 5 to 4 that the crèche violated the First Amendment. But in the same case, they voted 6 to 3 that it was constitutional to display the menorah next to the Christmas tree as part of a cultural exhibit.

By the time that the Supreme Court heard still another case about the prayer issue, in 1992, it had seven members who generally shared a conservative philosophy. Many Court analysts believed that a majority of justices would uphold a public school principal's decision to invite a rabbi to offer a prayer at graduation ceremonies. But three justices—Anthony M. Kennedy, Sandra Day O'Connor, and David H. Souter—deserted the conservative ranks to help create a 5 to 4 majority which decreed that the graduation prayer was contrary to the First Amendment.

These three justices, observed Harvard law professor Laurence Tribe, "have formed a moderate bloc that can control the Court."[1]

The following year, however, the Supreme Court showed it would not look with disfavor on all school prayers. Students at a high school in Houston, Texas, had voted to allow one of their members to deliver a nondenominational prayer at graduation ceremonies. A federal appeals court had decided that this student-initiated prayer did not violate the First Amendment, and the Supreme Court approved this ruling.

The Rehnquist Court in 1993 also approved the use of school facilities by religious groups for evening programs and the use of public funds to pay for a deaf student's sign-language interpreter at a religious school.

In 1994, the Court struck down a New York State law that had set up a publicly funded special school district for the disabled children of members of a Hasidic Jewish sect. The justices declared in this case that the government cannot financially support or show favoritism to institutions established by any religious group.

The 1993 decisions of the Rehnquist Court approving student-initiated school prayer, the evening use of school facilities by religious groups, and the payment of tax money for a deaf student's interpreter at a religious school represented a partial lowering of the wall separating church and state. On the other hand, the 1992 ruling against a rabbi's delivering a school prayer and the 1994 decision to close a special school district for the handicapped children belonging to a religious sect were Court judgments that overturned violations of the First Amendment.

THE FREE EXERCISE OF RELIGION

In the past forty years, the Supreme Court has considered fewer cases pertaining to the First Amendment's free exercise of religion clause than its establishment of religion clause.

The Warren Court decreed that a man of draft age who belongs to no church and acknowledges no belief in God but still holds strong religious convictions should be classified as a conscientious objector by his draft board. The Burger Court, however, ruled that a man cannot be exempted from the draft if his only opposition to military service is his belief that a particular war (such as the Vietnam War) is unjust.

Whether the children of parents who belonged to the Amish sect had to attend public school beyond the eighth grade was an issue settled by the Burger Court in 1972. The Amish claimed that public high school education promoted secular influences that conflicted with their strict religious beliefs. The Court agreed with the Amish and ordered that their children be exempted from compulsory school attendance laws. But the justices, by a 5 to 4 vote, ruled against an Air Force rabbi wearing a yarmulke (a Jewish skullcap) while on duty on the grounds that it conflicted with the armed forces' regulation that all of their personnel wear only the standard uniform.

For many years the Supreme Court followed the principle that persons could be exempted from a law that seriously interfered with their religious beliefs unless the state could prove that obeying this law served a compelling government interest. This principle was reviewed in a 1990 case by the Rehnquist Court. At issue was whether a Native American and his non–Native American friend who had ingested the drug peyote could be exempted from their state's drug laws because the use of peyote was part of their Native American church's religious ceremonies.

The justices voted 5 to 4 to overturn a lower court decision that the men's free exercise of religion had been violated. Furthermore, the Court broke with a long-established precedent by asserting that the banning of a religious practice need not be justified by a compelling government interest.

In another case, however, the Rehnquist Court in 1993 upheld a controversial practice by a religious minority. The followers of Santeria, an Afro-Cuban sect, killed various kinds of animals in Hialeah, Florida, as part of their religious ceremonies. This angered other people in Hialeah, and their city adopted an ordinance banning animal sacrifice. The Supreme Court unanimously voted in favor of the Santerians and struck down the ordinance that forbade the killing of animals in their religious ritual.

Regarding the free exercise of religion, the Rehnquist Court ended the judicial precedent that the banning of controversial religious practices must be justified by a compelling government interest.

SYMBOLIC SPEECH

The Warren Court heard some cases involving symbolic speech that arose as a result of the civil rights movement that accelerated in the 1960s. It unanimously upheld the right of blacks to hold sit-in demonstrations at lunch counters in the South that previously had been reserved for whites only. The Court also ruled in favor of student demonstrators who had assembled peacefully at the South Carolina statehouse to protest racial discrimination.

American participation in the Vietnam War triggered other major Warren Court decisions. A young man had been convicted for burning his draft card to protest the war and the draft, and he claimed that this action was an expression of symbolic speech protected by the First Amendment. The Supreme Court upheld the man's conviction, asserting that the draft registration system was an essential part of Congress's responsibility to raise and maintain armies. But the Court sustained the right of students in Des Moines, Iowa, to wear black armbands to school as a symbolic protest against the Vietnam War.

In 1969, during its last session, the Warren Court decided the first case in modern times regarding flag burning. A black man, reacting to the news of the shooting of civil rights leader James Meredith, had made degrading remarks about the U.S. flag as he burned it. He was convicted under a New York State law that made it a crime to mutilate an American flag or show it disrespect by words or conduct. By a 5 to 4 vote, the Court reversed the man's conviction on the grounds that he had been wrongly punished for his words, which were safeguarded by the First and Fourteenth Amendments. But the Warren Court did not resolve the question of whether burning the flag could also be constitutionally protected.

In two separate cases, the Burger Court dealt with bizarre, unorthodox displays of the flag. One case involved a man who wore a small flag on the seat of his pants; the other case involved flying the flag upside down. The Court upheld both of these practices as constitutionally protected expressions of symbolic speech.

A major flag-burning case was decided by the Rehnquist Court in 1989. The case pertained to a young member of a Communist group who had set fire to an American flag outside the 1984 Republican convention arena in Dallas, Texas. This was a violation of a Texas law that prohibited the deliberate destruction of the flag. The Court voted 5 to 4 to reverse the flag burner's conviction, ruling that while most Americans might despise the act of willfully destroying the flag, it was a permissible form of symbolic speech. Surprisingly, two conservative justices, Scalia and Kennedy, voted with the majority. Kennedy asserted that the First Amendment dictates that the government may not prohibit the expression of an idea that is "offensive or disagreeable."

Shortly after this decision, Congress passed the Flag Protection Act, making it illegal to knowingly mutilate, deface, or burn the flag. The Supreme Court, however, by the same 5 to 4 vote, declared this new law unconstitutional.

The Rehnquist Court ruled on a so-called hate crime case in 1992. A teenager had burned a wooden cross on the lawn of a black family's house. He was convicted under an ordinance that forbade placing on public or private property any symbol which represented racial or other forms of bigotry that could arouse anger, alarm, or resentment in others. Voting unanimously, the Supreme Court overturned the ordinance and declared that the government cannot punish those who communicate messages of intolerance simply because these messages express ideas that are offensive to many people. The Court suggested that the defendant should have been charged instead with arson or damage to property. This decision appeared to strike down many state laws and city ordinances that made it a criminal offense to burn a cross or to display a Nazi swastika or other bigotry-based messages on signs and T-shirts.

In 1993, the Rehnquist Court decided whether judges could impose longer prison terms on defendants whose physical assaults on innocent persons were motivated by their victims' race, religion, national origin, gender, or sexual orientation. The justices voted unanimously that a person who committed a hate-crime assault could be given a stiffer penalty than a person who was guilty of the same offense but whose conduct was not motivated by bigotry. Chief Justice Rehnquist explained that a physical assault was not symbolic speech protected by the First Amendment.

In a 1994 case, the Supreme Court unanimously struck down an ordinance that banned nearly all signs in Ladue, Missouri. The justices agreed that a woman in Ladue had the constitutional right to place on her lawn and in her house window signs protesting the Persian Gulf war.

Deciding that symbolic speech, as well as oral speech, was in most instances guaranteed by the First Amendment, the Rehnquist Court generally followed the precedents established by the Warren Court and the Burger Court. With the exception of the 5 to 4 vote in two flag-burning cases, the Rehnquist Court handed down unanimous decisions in other major symbolic speech cases.

CIVIL RIGHTS

The "separate but equal" doctrine established by the Supreme Court in the 1898 *Plessy* v. *Ferguson* decision legalized racial segregation for more than half a century. Finally, in 1954, one important aspect of racial discrimination was challenged when the Warren Court handed down its unanimous 1954 landmark decision in *Brown* v. *Board of Education of Topeka*. Chief Justice Warren declared, "We conclude that in the field of public education the doctrine of 'separate but equal' has no place. Separate educational facilities are inherently unequal."

This order by the Supreme Court to integrate public schools "represented nothing short of a reconsecration of American ideals," wrote Richard Kluger in his book *Simple Justice.*[2] But it sent a wrenching shock wave throughout the South, where blacks and whites traditionally had been educated in separate schools.

The *Brown* decision did not spell out how or when school integration was to be implemented, so the next year the Supreme Court considered these questions in a follow-up decision known as *Brown* II. Recognizing that radical changes in the public school systems in the entire South posed major problems that could not be solved immediately, the Court set no specific date for achieving integration but ordered the southern states to proceed with "all deliberate speed." This vague wording gave segregationists the opportunity to move very slowly in applying the Court mandate and to seek various ways to circumvent the integration of their schools.

In an effort to prevent integration, Prince Edward County in Virginia closed its public schools and used public funds to help finance private schools for white children. The High Court, by a vote of 7 to 2, ordered that the public schools must be reopened as integrated schools and that private schools cannot be operated with taxpayers' money.

While the two *Brown* rulings were limited to education, they opened the door to advancing civil rights in other areas. Congress passed sweeping civil rights bills in 1964, 1965, and 1968. All three of these measures were upheld as constitutional by the Warren Court.

School desegregation cases came to the attention of the Burger Court, too. In 1969, the Court voted unanimously to deny a request from thirty-three Mississippi school districts to delay indefinitely school integration—fifteen years after the first *Brown* decision. Two years later, the Court decreed that school districts could use various methods to achieve school desegregation, such as the busing of students, the racial balancing of schools, and the redrawing of school enrollment boundaries.

The Burger Court, however, struck down desegregation plans that it considered unreasonable. It reversed a plan calling for the busing of students among fifty-four Michigan school districts. It

also ruled that after a school board has established a racially balanced plan for assignment of students to its schools it does not have to continue shifting student enrollments in order to keep an exact racial balance in the student body of every school.

The Burger Court considered cases that resulted from affirmative action programs designed to create better jobs and educational opportunities for minorities, especially blacks, who were the victims of existing discrimination and the effects of past discrimination. In some instances, white persons protested that affirmative action programs denied them the equal protection of their rights and resulted in reverse discrimination.

Alan Bakke, a white man, sued a medical school for not admitting him while enrolling a specific quota of minority students—even though some of these students did not have qualifications as high as his. By 5 to 4 margins, the Burger Court handed down two decisions in this 1978 case. It ruled that Bakke's constitutional rights had been violated and ordered the medical school to admit him. It also ruled that affirmative action plans are constitutional but specific racial quotas are not.

Two Burger Court decisions in the 1980s struck down affirmative action plans that conflicted with valid seniority systems. One plan would have preserved the jobs of black firefighters who had less seniority than whites; the other plan would have caused white teachers with more seniority to be laid off to protect the teaching positions of blacks who had less seniority.

Soon after William Rehnquist became chief justice in 1986, the Supreme Court, by a vote of 5 to 4, upheld a judge's order that Alabama must promote one black state police officer for every white police officer promoted. Rehnquist was a dissenter in this case, but after the appointment of Anthony Kennedy to the Court in 1988, the chief justice usually had enough conservative votes to squelch controversial affirmative action plans.

Chief Justice Earl Warren wrote the
opinion in the historic unanimous
decision that said segregation of public
schools was unconstitutional (1954).

The Rehnquist Court struck down affirmative action programs for construction workers in Virginia and for firefighters in Alabama on the grounds that they violated the constitutional rights of whites. In another case, lawyers presented statistics showing that most Filipino workers at an Alaskan salmon cannery were excluded from higher-paying jobs. But the Rehnquist Court dismissed this claim and established a new precedent that minority employees cannot rely on statistics alone to prove that job policies are discriminatory.

Justice Byron White deserted the conservative bloc to provide the fifth vote in a case in which the Court upheld the Federal Communication Commission's decision to award a license for a new television station to a company owned by Hispanics instead of to a company controlled by whites. In a 1992 civil rights case, the Court ruled that lawyers cannot reject all potential black jurors in an effort to obtain an all-white jury. In the same year, the justices ordered that the state of Mississippi had not taken sufficient steps to dismantle its previously segregated system of public colleges and universities.

The most important 1993 civil rights cases provided setbacks for minority groups. By a 5 to 4 vote, the Rehnquist Court determined that a fired worker had to prove that the reason for being dismissed is intentional discrimination on the part of the employer. By the same 5 to 4 margin, the Court ruled that the North Carolina legislature had violated the constitutional rights of whites when it created a gerrymandered, irregularly drawn congressional district to improve the chance for a black candidate to be elected to the House of Representatives.

In 1994, the Court overturned a judge's order to redistrict the Florida House of Representatives in such a way as to create the greatest possible number of districts in which Hispanic voters in Dade County would constitute a majority.

In the area of civil rights, the Warren Court began the process of school desegregation and consistently ruled in favor of disadvantaged minorities. Both the Burger Court and the Rehnquist Court defended the rights of minorities in some cases. But in other rulings, especially those pertaining to affirmative action plans, they often voted to protect the rights of white people who claimed they were the victims of reverse discrimination.

ABORTION

Until the 1970s, states were generally free to establish their own regulations and restrictions regarding abortion. The abortion issue did not come before the Warren Court. But it did hear a major case pertaining to the right of privacy, even though this right is not mentioned in the Constitution or any of its amendments. In *Griswold* v. *Connecticut* (1965), the justices voted 7 to 2 to strike down a state law that forbade the use of contraceptives by anyone, including married couples.

Probably the best-known and most controversial decision made by the Burger Court was based on the *Roe* v. *Wade* case (1973). By a 7 to 2 vote, the Court overturned a Texas law banning abortion. In effect, this momentous ruling legalized abortion throughout the United States, but the Court also decreed that a woman's decision to end a pregnancy is not an absolute right. Writing for the majority, Justice Harry Blackmun explained that during the first three months of pregnancy a woman cannot be denied an abortion; during the next three months the state may impose some regulations but not ban abortion; during the final three months of pregnancy, when the fetus could probably live on its own outside the mother's body, the state can forbid an abortion, except when it is necessary to protect the health of the mother.

The *Roe* v. *Wade* decision set the stage for a fierce battle that is still raging between those who favor abortion (pro-choice groups) and those who oppose it (pro-life groups). Pro-choice advocates argue that the pregnant woman must have control of her body and the right to decide whether she will give birth. Pro-life supporters contend that abortion is a form of murder and that no one has the right to deny the birth of a child.

In 1986, the Burger Court decided a case that tested the constitutionality of a Pennsylvania law which required doctors to take several steps designed to discourage pregnant women from having abortions. The Court struck down this law by a close vote of 5 to 4. Since *Roe*, the number of justices supporting abortion had shrunk from seven to five.

The Burger Court was less activist than the Warren Court and less
traditionalist than the Rehnquist Court.

After abortion foe William Rehnquist had become chief justice, President Reagan in 1988 appointed to the Supreme Court
Anthony Kennedy, a conservative Catholic and presumably an
opponent of abortion. In 1989, the Rehnquist Court heard its
first major abortion case, *Webster* v. *Reproduction Health Services*.
It was based on a Missouri law that prohibited abortions in any
public hospital, forbade the use of public funds for abortion, and
ordered doctors to make tests showing whether the fetus could
probably live outside the mother's womb after she had been pregnant for twenty weeks. Voting 5 to 4 to uphold the Missouri law,
the Rehnquist Court dealt the pro-choice supporters their first judicial defeat in sixteen years.

The Court in 1990 considered two cases pertaining to abortion regulations imposed on pregnant teenagers. A Minnesota law required both parents be notified before a pregnant minor could have an abortion. By a 5 to 4 vote, the Court struck down this law because one parent might be absent or abusive, but it ordered that a minor who could not get the consent of both parents must obtain a judge's permission before proceeding with the abortion. In the other case, the Court upheld a Ohio law which said that a pregnant minor who had not notified either parent must persuade a judge that she was mature enough to have an abortion.

After two more justices, moderate David Souter and conservative Clarence Thomas, were added to the Court by President Bush, pro-life advocates felt that they now had enough justices on their side to reverse *Roe* entirely and return to the states the complete power to deal with this controversial subject. The opportunity to test this possibility occurred in 1992 when the Court ruled on a Pennsylvania law that contained many stringent regulations on the abortion procedure. The Rehnquist Court voted 5 to 4 to uphold nearly all the provisions in this law, but, at the same time, it reaffirmed *Roe* and the fundamental right of a woman to have an abortion. Court observers were astonished by this decision to retain *Roe*. It came about largely because Souter and two generally conservative justices—Kennedy and Sandra Day O'Connor—asserted that even if they personally believed abortion was wrong, they had no right to force their own moral codes on all American women.

Later, the Court struck down a Guam law that forbade nearly all abortions, but it upheld Mississippi and North Dakota statutes requiring a twenty-four-hour waiting period before doctors could perform abortions.

The abortion controversy heightened when some right-to-life supporters tried to blockade abortion clinics and at times resorted to acts of violence, such as assaults and arson. Various judges, relying on a civil rights act that Congress had passed in 1871 to protect blacks from white mobs, ordered an end to abortion clinic blockades and violent acts against pro-choice advocates. But in a 6 to 3 decision, the Supreme Court ruled in 1993 that this nineteenth century act could not be applied to abortion protests. In 1994, however, the Court decreed that judges could use an antiracketeering act passed in 1970 to curb "conspiracies" of pro-life groups that engaged in abortion clinic blockades and violent activities.

Congress enacted a law in 1994 forbidding abortion clinic blockades and threats or violence against the clinics. Anyone trying to blockade abortion clinic entrances would be committing a crime punishable by imprisonment, a fine, or both. Stiffer sentences would be given to abortion protesters who commit acts of violence.

The Supreme Court in 1994 upheld a court order creating a "protest-free" zone around an abortion clinic in Melbourne, Florida. This buffer zone was set up to protect the rights of patients and staff members to enter the clinic without fear of intimidation.

The Burger Court in its landmark *Roe* decision upheld the right of a woman to have an abortion. While the Rehnquist Court did not reverse this right, in several cases it approved various restrictions and regulations that state laws imposed on women seeking abortions.

SEX DISCRIMINATION

Spurred by the increasingly active civil rights and feminist movements, sex discrimination became a major issue in the courts in the 1970s. When the Burger Court in 1971 overturned an Idaho law giving preference to males as estate administrators, this was the first time in its history that the Supreme Court ruled that a law was unconstitutional because it discriminated against women. The Burger Court also struck down laws that permitted the automatic exemption of women from juries in Louisiana and that gave male members of the armed forces larger benefits for their families than it gave to female members.

Recognizing that sex discrimination can affect either gender, the Burger Court invalidated an Oklahoma law that banned the sale of 3.2 percent beer to men under the age of twenty-one but permitted its sale to women eighteen or older. The Court declared that a classification based on gender cannot be allowed unless it is substantially related to the achievement of an important governmental objective. The Burger Court, however, did not reverse all laws based on gender. It upheld the limitation of draft registration to males, and it sustained rape laws that punished underage males but not females.

In 1986, the Supreme Court decided its first sexual harassment case. The justices voted unanimously that sexual harassment in the workplace is illegal not only when it results in the loss of a job or a promotion, but also when it creates an offensive or hostile working environment.

The Rehnquist Court validated the right of women to become members of the previously all-male Rotary Club. By a 6 to 3 vote, it approved a woman's claim to a position as a road dispatcher as a result of her employer's affirmative action plan. The Court also upheld a California law that permitted women to regain their jobs after taking an unpaid disability leave to have a baby.

In a 1991 case, the Rehnquist Court decided whether pregnant women could continue working at jobs involving a high exposure to lead that could cause unplanned abortions or genetic defects in their children. By a 6 to 3 vote, the Court ruled that the pregnant women, not their employers, had the sole right to determine whether they would work under these conditions.

The Supreme Court considered the question of what constituted a hostile, abusive environment in a major sexual harassment case decided in 1993. In *Harris* v. *Forklift Systems*, Teresa Harris sued her employer for monetary damages, claiming that she had been subjected to offensive jokes, suggestions that she might have promised to have sex with a customer, and degrading remarks about being inferior because she was a woman. The Rehnquist Court ruled unanimously that Harris had been the victim of illegal sexual harassment and was entitled, under the Civil Rights Act of 1991, to receive damages from her employer. The Court explained that a person can win damages in a lawsuit by showing that she or he had suffered severe and persistent sexual harassment, regardless of whether the person's job performance or mental health had been affected.

In 1994, however, the Rehnquist Court decreed that the provisions of the Civil Rights Act of 1991 permitting sexual harassment victims to sue for damages did not apply to cases that had been decided before this law went into effect.

In another 1994 case, by a vote of 6 to 3, the Supreme Court declared that neither women nor men can be excluded from serving on juries because of their gender.

The precedents regarding sex discrimination cases established by the Burger Court have generally been followed and even expanded by the Rehnquist Court.

RIGHTS OF THE ACCUSED

The activist Warren Court established important precedents for protecting the rights of the accused. In *Gideon* v. *Wainwright* (1963), it extended the right of poor defendants to be represented by government-paid lawyers in state, as well as in federal, criminal trials. By a 5 to 4 vote in *Escobedo* v. *Illinois* (1964), the Court decreed that a suspect during a police interrogation has the right to have a lawyer and the right to remain silent.

In 1966, the justices voted 5 to 4 in the landmark case of *Miranda* v. *Arizona* to establish specific procedures that law enforcement officers must follow after arresting persons for possibly committing crimes. The *Miranda* rules include these protections for suspects: (1) before being questioned, they must be informed of their right to remain silent, (2) they must be told that anything they say can be used against them in court, (3) they have the right to be assisted by a lawyer during police interrogations, and (4) if they are too poor to afford an attorney, one will be appointed at government expense before the questioning begins. Any statements obtained without following these rules cannot be used in court as evidence against the defendants.

The Burger Court was somewhat less committed than the Warren Court to the protection of individual rights and somewhat more committed to the protection of society by law enforcement officers. In a 1971 case, the Burger Court decreed that voluntary statements made by a suspect who had not been told of his or her rights before being questioned by the police could still be used to question the suspect's truthfulness if, on the witness stand, the suspect contradicts the earlier statements.

A 1984 case dealt with the question of whether police must first advise a suspect of his or her *Miranda* rights in a situation in which public safety is at stake. While frisking Benjamin Quarles, who was suspected of committing a crime, police noticed his wearing a shoulder holster and asked where the gun was. Quarles replied that it was in a nearby carton. After the police seized the gun, they read him his *Miranda* rights. The Supreme Court, by a vote of 5 to 4, ruled that both the gun and Quarles's statement about it could be used as evidence against him because people nearby would have been in danger had an accomplice picked up the concealed weapon.

In a 1986 case, the Burger Court ruled that a confession to a crime is valid even if police fail to inform the suspect that an attorney wants to see him or her before the questioning begins.

The Rehnquist Court in 1990 decided two cases that involved the Sixth Amendment right of a person accused of a crime to be confronted with the prosecution witnesses. In one case, a preschool teacher had been accused of abusing children, who were permitted to testify via closed-circuit television because prosecution attorneys believed their testimony might be affected if they saw the teacher whom they allegedly feared. By a vote of 5 to 4, the Court upheld the woman's conviction. The other case involved an Idaho woman accused of abusing her own child. Testifying against her was a doctor who claimed the woman's two-year-old daughter had told him about being abused. The Court reversed the woman's conviction, saying there was insufficient proof that the statements made by the doctor were accurate or trustworthy, since he had no tape recording or notes to validate his secondhand charges.

The long-established Court principle that only confessions that are voluntary can be used as evidence was tested in a 1991 case. While Oreste Fulminante was imprisoned for another crime, he became afraid other inmates might attack him because of rumors that he had killed his young stepdaughter. Another prisoner, who was secretly an FBI informant, promised Fulminante protection if he would tell him whether these rumors were true. Fulminante then confessed to the murder. Later, he was convicted on the murder charge. His lawyers appealed that

Fulminante's confession had been coerced (forced) because he made it at a time when he feared that his life was endangered. The Rehnquist Court upheld his conviction by a vote of 5 to 4. Chief Justice Rehnquist, speaking for the majority, explained that coerced confessions do not invalidate the central purpose of a criminal trial, which is to determine the defendant's guilt or innocence.

In 1993, the Court ruled unanimously that a criminal defendant who deliberately lies in courtroom testimony may be subjected to a longer prison sentence as a result of having tried to obstruct justice. The following year, the Court was asked to review the case of a Montana man whose insanity appeal had been denied at his trial because the state of Montana had removed insanity as a defense from its criminal code. The Rehnquist Court did not strike down the Montana rule and permitted the defendant to be imprisoned for the crime.

Another 1994 case involved a a man who originally was not considered the chief suspect in a murder and voluntarily went with officers to a police station, where he willingly answered questions. When the police discovered from information he disclosed that he was the likely murderer, they quickly read him his *Miranda* rights. The man was convicted, but his attorneys appealed on the grounds that their client was in custody and subjected to questioning before he was told of his rights. The Supreme Court unanimously agreed that the *Miranda* rules had been violated. But instead of reversing the defendant's conviction, the justices ordered the lower court to restudy the case without using any trial evidence based on what the man said during the period when he had been illegally questioned.

Both the Burger Court and the Rehnquist Court weakened the *Miranda* rules established by the Warren Court and placed a higher priority on the rights and practices of law enforcement officers than on the rights of persons suspected of breaking laws. The Rehnquist Court also restricted the Sixth Amendment's guarantee that the defendant may always confront prosecution witnesses, and it overturned the long-standing judicial precedent that only voluntary confessions can be used as evidence in trials.

PROTECTION AGAINST
SEARCH AND SEIZURE

The Fourth Amendment's protection against searches and seizures has been the source of many Supreme Court cases in the past four decades. In the 1961 landmark case of *Mapp* v. *Ohio*, the Warren Court extended the exclusionary rule to include state courts as well as federal courts; this rule provided that illegally seized evidence must be excluded from a trial.

In most situations, law enforcement officers need to obtain a warrant to conduct a search, but the Supreme Court has permitted some exceptions to this rule. For example, in *Terry* v. *Ohio* (1968), the Court declared that the police practice of frisking suspicious persons to search for weapons is permissible without a search warrant.

The Warren Court dealt with the question of whether the Fourth Amendment also protected a suspect against eavesdropping. In a 1967 ruling, it banned warrantless eavesdropping. The following year, Congress passed a law legalizing eavesdropping by the police or the FBI only in those situations in which a warrant has been obtained from a judge or Justice Department official who agrees there is probable cause of criminal activity.

The Burger Court ruled in 1969 that when the police legally arrest a person, they must restrict their warrantless search to the immediate area around the suspect. A 1978 case involved police who had used a search warrant rather than a subpoena to inspect the offices of a Stanford University student newspaper for incriminating evidence, even though no one in the newsrooms was a suspect in the crime. The Supreme Court confirmed the police's right to use a search warrant in this situation.

In 1984, the Burger Court permitted the first exception to the exclusionary rule. It decreed that there are circumstances in which the prosecution may use evidence that was illegally obtained. In this case, the police had used a search warrant that later was found to be defective. The Burger Court also extended warrantless searches to include motor homes and aerial surveillances of property that might contain marijuana plants.

The Rehnquist Court heard a 1988 case about federal agents who first had searched a drug dealers' warehouse without a warrant, and, after finding marijuana inside, obtained a warrant to search for and seize the illegal drug. The justices agreed that the first search had been illegal, but they voted 4 to 3 to uphold the drug dealers' convictions on the grounds that the evidence of marijuana should not have been excluded from the trial simply because it was seen before the warrant was issued. In another 1988 case, the Court ruled that a warrantless search by police of the curbside garbage of a suspected drug dealer was permissible.

In 1989, the Supreme Court decided two cases pertaining to the warrantless search of persons for the consumption of drugs and alcohol. It upheld the Federal Railroad Administration's regulations that required drug and alcohol testing of railroad employees after a train accident. By a 5 to 4 vote, the Court approved the mandatory drug testing of U.S. Customs employees who applied for promotions to jobs involving possible drug shipments or the handling of information that might be useful to drug dealers.

The Rehnquist Court considered a 1990 case that raised the question of whether the ban on warrantless searches could be extended to foreign countries. Mexican police had arrested a man suspected of smuggling drugs into the United States and handed him over to U.S. marshals at the border crossing near San Diego. Then U.S. agents conducted a warrantless search at the suspect's two houses in Mexico and seized alleged records of drug shipments. By a 6 to 3 vote, the Supreme Court decreed that these records could be used as evidence.

In a 1993 case, the Rehnquist Court ruled that cocaine which was discovered without a warrant during a search for weapons could not be used as evidence against the defendant. Drugs were involved in two other 1993 cases that stemmed from a 1989 law permitting the government to seize any property that had been used in any way to help carry out a drug crime. Government agents had confiscated a South Dakota man's mobile home and automobile repair shop after he had been convicted for selling two grams of cocaine. The Court unanimously decided that this punishment was too severe and violated the defendant's Eighth Amendment protection against "cruel and unusual punishment" and "excessive fines."

In a somewhat similar case, federal agents had confiscated a house and land belonging to a man in Hawaii who previously had served in jail after marijuana had been discovered in his home. The Hawaiian man contended that his constitutional rights had been violated because his property had been seized without first notifying him and giving him the opportunity to present his objections at a court hearing before the seizure. By a vote of 5 to 4, the Supreme Court ruled in the man's favor, declaring that his right to prior notice and a court hearing are protected by the Constitution's due process clause.

The Warren Court insisted that the police or other government officers must obtain warrants to conduct most types of searches. Both the Burger Court and the Rehnquist Court permitted the use of evidence obtained without search warrants in some cases—especially those involving the possession and sale of drugs. Permitting evidence based on these warrantless searches was held to be justified on the grounds that the protection of society in some instances outweighed the defense of individual rights. The Rehnquist Court also approved the warrantless drug and alcohol testing of railroad workers after train accidents and U.S. Customs employees who were seeking promotions to positions dealing with drugs. The Court, however, decreed that the government's confiscation of drug dealers' property had to be reasonable and not in violation of protections guaranteed by the Constitution.

CAPITAL PUNISHMENT

The Warren Court ruled in 1968 that since every community has persons who oppose the death penalty, such persons cannot be banned as jurors in cases that might call for this form of punishment. Otherwise, juries would not represent the views of the entire community.

By a vote of 5 to 4, the Burger Court in 1972 struck down all existing death penalty laws on the grounds that they violated the Eighth Amendment and the Fourteenth Amendment. Two of the justices in the majority, William J. Brennan, Jr., and Thurgood Marshall, believed that capital punishment should be entirely prohibited in our modern, supposedly humane, society. Three other justices, William O. Douglas, Byron R. White, and Potter Stewart, objected to the death penalty because they felt it was unfairly imposed—some convicted criminals were put to death while others who committed similar crimes were given prison sentences.

Although executions were stopped in 1972, the Supreme Court permitted two procedures by which states could rewrite their death penalty laws. One procedure called for making capital punishment mandatory for certain specific crimes. The other procedure required lower courts to hold separate hearings involving the most serious crimes: the first hearing would determine whether the defendant was guilty, and, if the person was convicted, a second hearing would decide whether the death penalty would be applied.

Many states passed new capital punishment laws. The Burger Court generally overturned state laws requiring the death penalty for certain crimes—usually because they did not allow juries to consider any special circumstances pertaining to the crimes. But the Court approved most of the state laws that called for defendants to be given a separate sentence hearing after the original hearing established guilt.

The Rehnquist Court adopted a stern attitude toward defendants appealing the death sentence. In 1987, it established a new precedent that permitted accomplices in a murder case (as well as the actual murderers) to be executed. In another case, involving a black murderer of a white police officer in Georgia, the Court approved the death sentence, despite statistics showing that in this southern state killers of whites were much more likely to be executed than killers of blacks. Also, by 5 to 4 margins, the Supreme Court maintained that it was constitutional to give death sentences to murderers sixteen and seventeen years of age and to another murderer who was mentally retarded but had been found sufficiently competent to be tried in court.

In the 1990s, the Rehnquist Court has delivered decisions that strongly restrict the rights of prisoners on Death Row to have their cases reopened by habeas corpus appeals. These appeals permit federal judges to hear prisoners' claims that either errors had been made during their trials in state courts or that new evidence had been uncovered which might prove their innocence. Conservative justices on the Rehnquist Court believe that the habeas corpus process is being abused; they maintain that federal judges are being deluged by many appeals that are not appropriate and delay just punishment for the condemned.

One habeas corpus case that was decided by the Supreme Court in 1991 pertained to a convicted murderer whose lawyer claimed to have newly discovered evidence but filed his appeal one day after the allotted time limit had expired. The Court, by a 6 to 3 vote, asserted that missing the deadline for filing the claim prohibited the federal judge from considering the appeal.

A 1993 case involved a man who was sentenced to death for the murder of two police officers in 1982. Nearly ten years after the crime was committed, witnesses came forward to say that the condemned man's brother, who died in 1984, was the murderer. The state court, believing that this supposedly new evidence was not true, refused to reopen the case. Then the defendant's lawyers filed a habeas corpus claim that was rejected.

The Supreme Court, by a 6 to 3 vote, ruled that the long-delayed statements by the witnesses were not trustworthy and upheld the man's death sentence. Chief Justice Rehnquist, speaking for the majority, declared that the power to determine the guilt or innocence of a person lies with the trial jury. He said that a federal judge cannot intervene unless the state court violates constitutional procedures or new evidence is presented in a "truly extraordinary" case which shows that the convicted defendant is unquestionably innocent of the charges.

In 1994, the Supreme Court took the unusual step of striking down a death penalty because the trial jury had not been informed of its options before determining the sentence of a convicted man. The defendant in this South Carolina case had been found guilty of three serious crimes, and, according to that state's law, persons convicted of this many major crimes would be imprisoned for life without parole if not given the death penalty. But neither the judge nor the prosecutors had explained to the jury that under no circumstances would this criminal ever be set free. So the Rehnquist Court reversed the defendant's death sentence on the grounds that the state had not provided the jury with accurate information which might have caused the jurors to change the punishment from death to life imprisonment.

The Court ruled in 1994 that federal judges may postpone a convict's execution while the defendant is trying to find a lawyer who will prepare a habeas corpus petition to be filed in a federal court. In another 1994 case, the Court upheld the California death penalty law against charges that under this law instructions to jurors are too vague and involve a variety of factors that are to be weighed when the jurors consider imposing the death sentence.

The Rehnquist Court took strong steps to buttress the justice system against claims that convicted criminals often were coddled and death penalties were unduly delayed. It ruled that accomplices in murder cases, defendants as young as sixteen, and mentally retarded persons could be executed. The Court also tightened the regulations governing the use of habeas corpus appeals made by defendants to federal judges after state appeals had failed.

MEMBERS OF THE REHNQUIST COURT

After Chief Justice Warren E. Burger resigned in 1986, President Ronald Reagan nominated Associate Justice William H. Rehnquist to fill this vacancy. When the Senate confirmed this appointment in September, Rehnquist became the third sitting associate justice in history to be elevated to the chief justiceship.

A native of Milwaukee, Wisconsin, Rehnquist graduated first in his class at Stanford Law School. Then he served for one year as a law clerk to Supreme Court justice Robert H. Jackson. Later, he practiced law in Arizona and became involved in Republican political campaigns. He moved to Washington, D.C., in 1968 to assume the position of assistant attorney general in charge of the Office of Legal Counsel. In 1971, President Richard M. Nixon appointed Rehnquist a justice of the Supreme Court.

From the moment he joined the Court, Rehnquist has argued consistently and vigorously in behalf of a very conservative approach to the interpretation of the Constitution. He usually has judged conflicts between an individual and the government in favor of the government, and he has been very reluctant to find federal and state laws unconstitutional. Rehnquist has been especially forceful in trying to limit the rights of defendants in criminal cases, while expanding the rights of the police and other law enforcement officers. He has repeatedly sought to find the original meanings intended by the Founding Fathers when they conceived the Constitution to use as guidelines in applying the provisions of that document to current cases.

Most conservatives have applauded Rehnquist's reasoning, while liberals have claimed that he is out of touch with current problems and changing values. Journalists Bob Woodward and Scott Anderson declared that when Rehnquist joined the Court, "he was prepared to turn the clock back a century."[1]

At the time that Rehnquist assumed leadership of the Court, the associate justices, ranked by seniority, were William J. Brennan, Jr., Byron R. White, Thurgood Marshall, Harry A. Blackmun, Lewis F. Powell, Jr., John Paul Stevens, Sandra Day O'Connor, and Antonin Scalia. All but three of these justices—Stevens, O'Connor, and Scalia—had longer seniority on the High Court than Rehnquist had.

William J. Brennan, Jr., was the only member of the Rehnquist Court appointed by President Dwight D. Eisenhower. He had been serving on the Court thirty years when Rehnquist was named chief justice.

The second of eight children of poor Irish Catholic parents who immigrated to the United States, Brennan was born in Newark, New Jersey. He displayed outstanding academic ability and graduated with honors from the University of Pennsylvania Wharton School of Finance and Harvard Law School. Brennan joined a prominent law firm and specialized in labor law. In 1949, he became a superior court judge, and in 1952 he was named to the New Jersey Supreme Court. When President Eisenhower selected him for the High Court in 1956, there was some criticism that Republican Eisenhower took this step to help win the votes of Catholic Democrats in his reelection race that year, but these charges were weakened by Brennan's established integrity and nonpolitical background.[2]

Activist Brennan and traditionalist Rehnquist usually were on opposite sides in cases involving the interpretation of the Bill of Rights and the Fourteenth Amendment. A holdover from the liberal Warren Court, Brennan consistently displayed a deep commitment to guaranteeing individual rights and civil liberties.

During the years when Earl Warren had been chief justice, Brennan wrote a large number of the Court's majority opinions, but as a member of the Rehnquist Court, he generally wrote dissenting opinions. He retired from the Court in 1990.

Byron R. White was the only member of the Rehnquist Court appointed by President John F. Kennedy. Born in Fort Collins, Colorado, White attended the University of Colorado, where he graduated first in his class. Known by the nickname "Whizzer," White won All-American honors as a football running back. After college, he divided his time between studying as a Rhodes Scholar at Oxford in England, pursuing a law degree at Yale Law School, and playing professional football for the Pittsburgh Steelers and later the Detroit Lions.

While a student at Oxford, White met Kennedy, whose father then was the U.S. ambassador to Great Britain. The two men renewed their acquaintance when both of them served in the South Pacific in World War II. In 1960, Kennedy ran for president; White headed his primary campaign in Colorado and later became chairman of the National Citizens for Kennedy organization. After the election, President Kennedy named White to the post of deputy attorney general, a position he held until appointed to the Supreme Court in 1962.

As a justice, White was a strong advocate of law and order, and he interpreted the rights of persons accused of crimes more narrowly than some other Court members. He generally believed that social problems should be solved by other branches of the national government and by the states. On the other hand, White usually supported disadvantaged individuals in cases involving racial discrimination, voting rights, and educational opportunity. White stepped down from the Court in 1993, after thirty-one years of service.

In 1967, President Lyndon B. Johnson appointed to the Supreme Court Thurgood Marshall, the first African-American justice. The son of a primary school teacher and a private club steward, Marshall was born in Baltimore, Maryland. He attended all-black Lincoln University in Chester, Pennsylvania, and helped finance his education by working as a grocery clerk and waiter. Marshall earned a reputation in college as an excellent debater.

He studied law at all-black Howard University in Washington, D.C., where he graduated first in his class.

During his law school years, Marshall developed a special interest in civil rights, and in time he became probably the foremost civil rights attorney in the United States. For many years Marshall served as head of the Legal Defense Fund of the National Association for the Advancement of Colored People (NAACP). He argued many cases before the Supreme Court, including *Brown* v. *Board of Education of Topeka*, in which the Court ruled school segregation unconstitutional (see Chapter 4).

In 1961, President Kennedy nominated Marshall to be a judge on the Court of Appeals for the Second Circuit, and in 1965 President Johnson chose him to be the nation's first black solicitor general. (The solicitor general represents the federal government as its chief advocate, or attorney, in cases before the Supreme Court.)

After Marshall joined the High Court, he was guided by the same dedication to racial justice and the rights of poor people that he had shown as an attorney. He wrote some important majority opinions, but as the Court became more conservative under both Chief Justice Burger and Chief Justice Rehnquist, he usually found himself part of a shrinking minority. After twenty-four years of service, Marshall retired from the Court in 1991.

Harry A. Blackmun was appointed to the Supreme Court by President Richard M. Nixon in 1970. Blackmun grew up in St. Paul, Minnesota, and one of his closest friends from primary school days was Warren E. Burger, with whom he was later to serve on the High Court. As a youth, Blackmun considered a career in medicine but chose instead to enter the field of law. He worked his way through Harvard Law School, doing a variety of jobs, including tutoring in math and driving the launch for the college crew team.

Chief Justice William H. Rehnquist
takes a very conservative approach to
the interpretation of the Constitution.

After law school, Blackmun practiced as an attorney in Minneapolis for sixteen years before leaving his law firm in 1950 to become counsel for the Mayo Clinic in Rochester, Minnesota. In 1959, President Eisenhower named Blackmun to the bench of the Eighth Circuit Court of Appeals. There he served for eleven years, earning a reputation as a capable, scholarly judge.

When a vacancy on the Supreme Court occurred in 1969, President Nixon twice named southerners—Clement Haynsworth of South Carolina and later Judge G. Harrold Caswell of Florida—to fill this position. But the Senate refused to confirm either of these appointees, so, on his third try, Nixon nominated Blackmun, who was confirmed unanimously by the Senate.

Blackmun and his childhood friend, Burger, soon became known as the Court's "Minnesota Twins" because in Blackmun's first years on the bench the two men tended to vote alike, usually siding with the conservative wing. Gradually, however, Blackmun began moving in a more liberal direction. He is best known for writing the majority opinion in *Roe* v. *Wade*, the decision that upheld the right of a woman to have an abortion (see Chapter 5). Following the resignations of Justices Brennan and Marshall, Blackmun emerged as the Court's most liberal member. After twenty-four years of service, Blackmun resigned from the Court in 1994.

On the same day in 1971 when President Nixon appointed Rehnquist as an associate justice, he nominated Lewis F. Powell, Jr., as another associate justice. Powell spent his childhood in Richmond, Virginia, and earned both an undergraduate degree and a law degree at Washington and Lee University in Lexington, Virginia. While practicing law for nearly forty years, Powell served on the board of directors of eleven large companies and as chairman of the Richmond school board, where he took a moderate stance during the bitter controversy over school desegregation in the South. He was highly respected by his fellow attorneys, who elected him president of the American Bar Association and of the American College of Trial Lawyers.

On the High Court, Powell acquired a reputation as a moderate justice. He often voted to uphold state laws and tended to favor the prosecution in cases against criminal defendants. But he took a middle-ground position on the issues of civil rights and individual liberties. Powell cast the deciding vote in many cases. In 1978, he provided the critical fifth vote against rigid race-based quotas in admission to a medical school, but in the same case he voted (with a different majority) to allow race as one of a number of factors that could be considered by a professional school in deciding which students to admit (see Chapter 4). Powell stepped down from the bench in 1987.

During his brief term in the White House, President Gerald Ford made only one appointment to the Supreme Court: John Paul Stevens in 1975. Stevens came from Chicago, Illinois, and graduated with honors from the University of Chicago in 1941. After serving as a naval officer in World War II, he earned a law degree at Northwestern University and then served as a law clerk to Supreme Court justice Wiley Rutledge. Returning to Chicago, he joined a prominent law firm and specialized in antitrust cases. In 1970, President Nixon appointed Stevens as a judge on the Seventh Circuit Court of Appeals, where he acquired a reputation as an insightful, scholarly member.

Ever since he joined the Supreme Court, Stevens has been described as an independent thinker who could not easily be classified as either conservative or liberal. Like Justice Powell, he has been considered a Court moderate, or centrist, but in recent years he has voted more often with the activist minority than with the traditionalist majority. Court analyst Robert J. Wagman said of Stevens's role on the Court, "His entire tenure has been marked by his independence, and his willingness to go it alone in a dissent or a concurring opinion if he does not agree with the majority. His moderate position has changed little," Wagman declared, "but he has found himself shifted from the philosphical right to the left as the Court has become more conservative."[3]

In 1981, President Ronald Reagan nominated the first woman justice in the history of the Supreme Court, Sandra Day O'Connor, and the largely male Senate confirmed her nomination unanimously. Sandra Day was born in El Paso, Texas, but her parents owned a large ranch in Arizona, where she spent much of her youth. She earned both her undergraduate degree and law degree at Stanford University. At the law school, she met two men who were to play important roles in her life—John J. O'Connor, whom she married in 1952, and William H. Rehnquist, whom she joined as a colleague on the Supreme Court.

O'Connor began her legal career as a deputy county attorney in San Mateo, California. Later, she moved with her husband and three children to Arizona, where she became an assistant attorney general in 1965. Four years later, she was appointed to fill a vacancy in the Arizona Senate, and she was elected to two subsequent terms. (O'Connor is the only member of the Rehnquist Court to win an elective office in a legislature.) She served for two years as majority leader of the Arizona Senate—the first woman in the United States to hold this high position of leadership. In 1975, O'Connor was elected a judge of the superior court in Arizona's Maricopa County. Four years later, she was elevated to the Arizona Court of Appeals and held this position until her appointment to the U.S. Supreme Court in 1981.

On the High Court, O'Connor has generally followed conservative principles. As a traditionalist, she has displayed a high respect for upholding Court precedents and has usually voted to protect the rights of states against interference by the federal government. She has remained independent, however, on some issues, particularly women's rights, and in cases dealing with these issues she has sometimes voted with the Court liberals.

At the time that President Reagan promoted Rehnquist to the chief justiceship in 1986, he appointed Antonin Scalia to replace Rehnquist as an associate justice. The first Supreme Court justice of Italian ancestry, Scalia was born in Trenton, New Jersey, and grew up in New York City, where he attended Jesuit schools. He acquired degrees at Georgetown University and Harvard Law School, and then was a practicing attorney in Cleveland, Ohio, for seven years. From 1968 to 1971, Scalia taught at the University of Virginia Law School.

An ardent Republican, Scalia served during the presidential terms of Nixon and Ford in a series of administrative positions, including assistant attorney general in charge of the Office of Legal Counsel. When Jimmy Carter recaptured the presidency for the Democrats in 1977, Scalia left Washington and taught for five years at the University of Chicago Law School. In 1982,

President Reagan appointed him to the U.S. Court of Appeals for the District of Columbia Circuit, where he remained for four years until Reagan selected him for the Supreme Court.

Like Rehnquist, Scalia has been a very conservative justice. Again and again he has opposed the efforts of activist colleagues to use the Court as a vehicle for bringing about social changes and protecting individual rights that he believes are not implied in the Constitution. A brilliant thinker and eloquent author, Scalia has written many concurrent opinions that accept the conclusions of the conservative bloc but not its reasoning.

President Reagan's final candidate for the Supreme Court was Anthony M. Kennedy, who was nominated in November 1987 and confirmed unanimously by the Senate in February 1988. Kennedy was born in Sacramento, California. He graduated from Stanford University, studied a year at the London School of Economics, and gained his law degree at Harvard Law School. He practiced law in California for fourteen years, until President Ford named him to the Ninth Court of Appeals in 1976. Kennedy served as an appellate judge for twelve years before his appointment to the Supreme Court.

Like Scalia, Kennedy is a Republican and a Roman Catholic. An advocate of judicial restraint, he usually votes with the Court's conservative wing. In his first year as a justice, he voted with Rehnquist in 92 percent of the cases, but in later years he has played a somewhat more independent role. To the astonishment of many Court observers, in 1992 he voted against the conservative position in a major school prayer case and in an important case that preserved a woman's right to have an abortion.

President George Bush's first appointment to the High Court was David H. Souter in 1990. Born in Melrose, Massachusetts, Souter moved as a youth to New Hampshire, where he spent most of his life before joining the Supreme Court. After graduating from Harvard University, he studied a year as a Rhodes Scholar in Oxford, England, and then returned to Harvard to earn his law degree at its law school. His private law practice lasted only two years before he accepted a position in the state attorney general's office in New Hampshire. Rising through the ranks in that office, he became state attorney general in 1976.

Two years later, Souter began his distinguished career as a judge, first presiding over a superior court and then being elevated in 1983 to the New Hampshire Supreme Court. President Bush named Souter to the U.S. Court of Appeals in 1990 and a few months later promoted him to the Supreme Court.

At the time of his appointment to the nation's highest court, Souter was called a "stealth justice" because little was known about where he stood on most issues. In the first year after he took his seat on the bench, he usually sided with the conservative bloc, but in subsequent years he has taken a more independent stance. According to Court observer Robert J. Wagman, ". . . Souter gradually emerged as a genuine intellectual force in the center of the Court—a balance to Scalia on the right. . . [He] seems to be staking out a role for himself as the centrist conscience of the Court; a role much like that played for many years by Justice Lewis Powell until his retirement in 1987."[4]

After Justice Marshall retired from the Court in 1991, President Bush named another African American, Clarence Thomas, to replace him. Thomas had overcome enormous handicaps in his rise from obscurity to prominence on the national stage. Born into an impoverished family in Pin Point, Georgia, he spent his first years living in a one-room wooden shack that had a dirt floor and no plumbing or electricity. Thomas attended Catholic elementary and secondary schools, where he studied diligently and earned high grades. Later, he worked his way through Holy Cross College and Yale University Law School.

After earning his law degree, Thomas joined the staff of Missouri's Republican attorney general, John Danforth, in 1974. Leaving government service temporarily, Thomas practiced corporate law for two years and then went to work again for Danforth, who had become a U.S. senator. Shortly after Ronald Reagan assumed the presidency in 1981, Thomas was appointed assistant secretary for civil rights in the Education Department. The next year he was named head of the Equal Employment Opportunity Commission, the nation's chief antidiscrimination agency, where he served for eight years. In March 1990, President

Bush nominated Thomas to the Court of Appeals for the District of Columbia and the following year to the Supreme Court.

Even though the president declared that Thomas was the best-qualified person to replace Marshall, strong objections to his appointment were raised. His critics charged that he had not had enough experience as either a judge or a practicing attorney to sit on the High Court. A committee of the American Bar Association that studies the qualifications of proposed justices rated Thomas as qualified but not well qualified (most proposed justices were rated well qualified). Thomas's critics claimed that his views were extremely conservative, but in his Senate confirmation hearings he refused to answer any questions pertaining to controversial issues.

Shortly before the Senate Judiciary Committee was scheduled to vote on whether to recommend Thomas's confirmation to the full Senate, the hearings had to be reopened to consider charges that Thomas might have sexually harassed one of his former female employees. The hearings on this complaint were aired dramatically on national television, and the public was divided regarding Thomas's guilt or innocence. Finally, the Senate accepted the appointment of Thomas to the Supreme Court by a 52 to 48 vote, the narrowest margin of approval in this century for a nominee to the nation's highest court.

As expected, Thomas allied with the other conservatives on the Court. A quiet, reserved man, he seldom asks questions or expresses opinions when lawyers are presenting oral arguments before the justices. But he nearly always votes on cases the same way that Scalia and Rehnquist do.

With the departure of Justice White from the bench in 1993, President Bill Clinton had his first opportunity to nominate a Supreme Court justice. He selected Ruth Bader Ginsburg, the second woman named to the Court and the first Jewish member since 1969. Ruth Bader was born in Brooklyn, New York, and acquired her undergraduate degree at Cornell University. She entered Harvard Law School and spent two years there before transferring to Columbia Law School to be with her husband, Martin, also a law student.

After earning her law degree in 1959, Ginsburg experienced discrimination against women attorneys when not one of the law firms in New York City to which she applied offered her employment. So in 1963 she launched a teaching career, instructing law students first at Rutgers University in New Jersey and later at her alma mater, Columbia Law School.

During the 1970s, Ginsburg acquired a national reputation as an outstanding attorney in the field of sex discrimination lawsuits. Representing the Women's Rights Project of the American Civil Liberties Union before the Supreme Court, she argued and won several major sex discrimination cases. These cases were brought on behalf of men almost as frequently as on behalf of women. For example, Ginsburg argued that women should be required to pay alimony to divorced husbands whose earnings were less than those of their former wives, and that a Florida law providing tax benefits to widows either had to be extended to widowers or overturned.

In 1980, President Carter appointed Ginsburg a judge on the Court of Appeals for the District of Columbia Circuit. During her thirteen-year service as an appellate judge, she was considered a moderate, sometimes voting with her conservative colleagues and other times with the liberals. When Ginsburg was promoted to the Supreme Court in 1993, it was widely predicted that she would vote to uphold women's rights and a strict separation of church and state, but take a middle-of-the-road position on most other issues.

After Justice Blackmun announced that he was stepping down from the bench in 1994, President Clinton appointed Judge Stephen G. Breyer as his replacement. Born the son of a San Francisco lawyer, Breyer earned his undergraduate degree at Stanford University. Before going on to Harvard Law School, he spent two years studying at Oxford University.

Justice Arthur J. Goldberg selected Breyer to serve as a clerk for the Supreme Court during its 1964–65 term. For the next several years, Breyer was employed in the Justice Department's antitrust division. Then he returned to Harvard to teach law courses. But in 1973 he spent several months in Washington, D.C., working on the Watergate investigation as an aide to special prosecutor Archibald Cox.

In 1974, Breyer accepted an offer by Senator Edward M. Kennedy to head the staff of the Senate Judiciary subcommittee on administrative law. Five years later, he became the Judiciary Committee's chief counsel. Committee members from both political parties praised Breyer for his fairness, knowledge of the law, and exceptional ability to forge a consensus (agreement) by bringing together persons with opposing beliefs.

In 1980, President Carter appointed Breyer a judge on the First Circuit Court of Appeals in Boston. Ten years later, he became chief judge of that court. While serving as a judge, Breyer continued to teach at Harvard and also played an important role on the U.S. Sentencing Commission, which worked to end the wide differences in sentences imposed by federal judges for similar crimes.

Court observers have predicted that Breyer will be a moderate justice, perhaps leaning to the liberal side in cases involving individual rights and civil rights. However, most of his beliefs—like Justice Ginsburg's—are generally considered to be middle of the road. His superb consensus-building skills may enable Breyer to become one of the most effective justices on the Supreme Court.

SOURCE NOTES

CHAPTER 1
1. Carl T. Rowan, *Dream Makers, Dream Breakers: The World of Justice Thurgood Marshall* (Boston: Little, Brown, 1993), p. 319.
2. Ibid., pp. 319–320.

CHAPTER 2
1. Nat Hentoff, *The First Freedom: The Tumultuous History of Free Speech in America* (New York: Dell, 1980), p. 164.
2. Leo Pfeffer, *Church, State and Freedom* (Boston: Beacon Press, 1967), p. 466.
3. Stephen Goode, *The Controversial Court: Supreme Court Influences on American Life* (New York: Messner, 1982), p. 95.
4. Hentoff, *The First Freedom*, p. 156.
5. John Leo, "A Secular Christmas to All," *U.S. News and World Report*, December 28, 1992, p. 31.
6. *New York Times*, November 4, 1992, p. A8.

CHAPTER 3
1. *Time*, July 3, 1989, p. 15.
2. *Newsweek*, July 3, 1989, p. 18.
3. Ibid.
4. *U.S. News and World Report*, July 10, 1989, p. 20.

5. Ibid., July 3, 1989, p. 28.
6. *Time*, July 3, 1989, p. 15.
7. Ibid.
8. Ibid., April 26, 1993, p. 31.

CHAPTER 4

1. G. Theodore Mitau, *Decade of Decision: The Supreme Court and the Constitutional Revolution, 1954-64* (New York: Scribner, 1967), pp. 62–63.
2. C. Vann Woodward, *The Strange Case of Jim Crow* (New York: Oxford University Press, 1966), p. 154.
3. Carl T. Rowan, *Dream Makers, Dream Breakers: The World of Justice Thurgood Marshall* (Boston: Little, Brown, 1993), p. 277.
4. John Morton Blum, *Years of Discord: American Politics and Society, 1961–1974* (New York: Norton, 1991), p. 192.
5. Richard Kluger, *Simple Justice* (New York: Knopf, 1976), p. 750.
6. Elder Witt, *The Supreme Court and Individual Rights*, 2d ed. (Washington, D.C.: Congressional Quarterly, 1988), p. 263.
7. David G. Savage, *Turning Right: The Making of the Rehnquist Supreme Court* (New York: Wiley, 1992), p. 334.

CHAPTER 5

1. Eric Foner and John A. Garraty, eds. *The Reader's Companion to American History* (Boston: Houghton Mifflin, 1991), p. 3.
2. Bob Woodward and Scott Armstrong, *The Brethren: Inside the Supreme Court* (New York: Simon and Schuster, 1979), p. 238.
3. Ibid.
4. *Newsweek*, July 17, 1989, p. 27.
5. *Los Angeles Times*, May 13, 1994, p. Al.
6. Ibid.
7. *USA Today*, July 1, 1994, p. 3A.
8. *New York Times*, July 1, 1994, p. A9.

CHAPTER 6

1. Jethro K. Lieberman, *The Evolving Constitution: How the Supreme Court Has Ruled on Issues from Abortion to Zoning* (New York: Random House, 1992), p. 488.

2. John Morton Blum, *Years of Discord: American Politics and Society, 1961–1974* (New York: Norton, 1991), p. 192.
3. Wendy W. Williams, "Sex Discrimination: Closing the Law's Gender Gap," in Herman Schwartz, ed., *The Burger Years: Rights and Wrongs in the Supreme Court, 1969–1986* (New York: Penguin Books, 1988), p. 114.
4. Timothy M. Phelps and Helen Winternitz, *Capitol Games: Clarence Thomas, Anita Hill, and the Story of a Supreme Court Nomination* (New York: Hyperion, 1992), p. 422.
5. *USA Today*, October 13, 1993, p. 2A.
6. *Los Angeles Times*, April 20, 1994, p. A19.

CHAPTER 7

1. *U.S. News and World Report*, March 22, 1993, p. 19.
2. John Morton Blum, *Years of Discord: American Politics and Society, 1961–1974* (New York: Norton, 1991), p. 207.
3. Ibid., p. 213.

CHAPTER 8

1. *The Supreme Court at Work* (Washington, D.C.: Congressional Quarterly, 1990), p. 255.
2. David G. Savage, *Turning Right: The Making of the Rehnquist Court* (New York: Wiley, 1992), p. 229.

CHAPTER 9

1. "Does the Criminal Justice System Discriminate Against African-Americans?" *Bill of Rights in Action* (Los Angeles: Constitutional Rights Foundation, Winter, 1992), p. 7.
2. *Time*, July 10, 1989, p. 49.
3. Ibid., p. 48.
4. *U.S. News and World Report*, May 24, 1993, p. 11.

CHAPTER 10

1. *Los Angeles Times*, July 1, 1992, p. A14.
2. Richard Kluger, *Simple Justice* (New York, Knopf, 1976), p. 710.

APPENDIX

1. Bob Woodward and Scott Anderson, *The Brethren: Inside the Supreme Court* (New York: Simon and Schuster, 1979), p. 221.
2. *The Supreme Court at Work* (Washington, D.C.: Congressional Quarterly, 1990), p. 199.
3. Robert J. Wagman, *The Supreme Court: A Citizen's Guide* (New York: Pharos Books, 1993), p. 262.
4. Ibid., p. 265.

FOR FURTHER READING

Bartholomew, Paul C. and Joseph F. Menez. *Summaries of Leading Cases on the Constitution.* Totowa, N.J.: Rowman and Allanheld, 1983.

Blasi, Vincent, ed. *The Burger Court: The Counter-Revolution That Wasn't.* New Haven, Conn.: Yale University Press, 1983.

Blum, John Morton. *Years of Discord: American Politics and Society, 1961-1974.* New York: Norton, 1991.

Boles, Donald E. *Mr. Justice Rehnquist, Judicial Activist.* Ames, Iowa: Iowa State University Press, 1987.

Cox, Archibald. *The Court and the Constitution.* Boston: Houghton Mifflin, 1987.

Coy, Harold. *The Supreme Court.* New York: Franklin Watts, 1981.

David, Andrew. *Famous Supreme Court Cases.* Minneapolis: Lerner, 1980.

Davis, Derek. *Original Intent: Chief Justice Rehnquist and the Course of American Church-State Relations.* Buffalo, N.Y.: Prometheus, 1991.

Forte, David F. *The Supreme Court.* New York: Franklin Watts, 1979.

Friedman, Leon. *The Supreme Court.* New York: Chelsea House, 1987.

Goode, Stephen. *The Controversial Court: Supreme Court Influences on American Life*. New York: Messner, 1982.

Harrell, Mary Ann, and Burnett Anderson. *Equal Justice under Law: The Supreme Court in American Life*. Washington, D.C.: Supreme Court Historical Society, 1982.

Hentoff, Nat. *The First Freedom: The Tumultuous History of Free Speech in America*. New York: Dell, 1981.

Irons, Peter. *The Courage of Their Convictions*. New York: Free Press, 1988.

Lieberman, Jethro K. *The Evolving Constitution: How the Supreme Court Has Ruled on Issues from Abortion to Zoning*. New York: Random House, 1992.

Lytle, Clifford M. *The Warren Court and Its Critics*. Tucson: University of Arizona Press, 1968.

O'Brien, David M. *Storm Center: The Supreme Court in American Politics*. New York: Norton, 1986.

Pfeffer, Leo. *Religion, State, and the Burger Court*. Buffalo, N.Y.: Prometheus, 1984.

Phelps, Timothy M., and Helen Winternitz. *Capitol Games: Clarence Thomas, Anita Hill, and the Story of a Supreme Court Nomination*. New York: Hyperion, 1992.

Rehnquist, William. *The Supreme Court: How It Was, How It Is*. New York: Morrow, 1987.

Rowan, Carl T. *Dream Makers, Dream Breakers: The World of Justice Thurgood Marshall*. Boston: Little, Brown, 1993.

Savage, David G. *Turning Right: The Making of the Rehnquist Court*. New York: Wiley, 1992.

Schwartz, Bernard, and Stephan Lesher. *Inside the Warren Court, 1953-1969*. Garden City, N.Y.: Doubleday, 1983.

Schwartz, Herman, ed. *The Burger Years: Rights and Wrongs in the Supreme Court, 1969-1986*. New York: Penguin Books, 1988.

Sgroi, Peter. *Blue Jeans and Black Robes: Teenagers and the Supreme Court*. New York: Messner, 1979.

Spaeth, Harold J. *The Warren Court: Cases and Commentary*. San Francisco: Chandler, 1966.

The Supreme Court at Work. Washington, D.C.: Congressional Quarterly, 1990.

The Supreme Court of the United States: Its Beginnings and Its Justices, 1790-1991. Washington, D.C.: Commission on Bicentennial of the Constitution, 1992.

Tribe, Laurence H. *God Save This Honorable Court: How the Choice of Supreme Court Justices Shapes Our History.* New York: Random House, 1985.

Wagman, Robert J. *The Supreme Court: A Citizen's Guide.* New York: Pharos Books, 1993.

Weiss, Ann E. *The Supreme Court.* Hillside, N.J.: Enslow, 1987.

Witt, Elder. *A Different Justice: Reagan and the Supreme Court.* Washington, D.C.: Congressional Quarterly, 1986.

——. *The Supreme Court and Individual Rights*, 2d ed. Washington, D.C.: Congressional Quarterly, 1988.

Woodward, Bob, and Scott Armstrong. *The Brethren: Inside the Supreme Court.* New York: Simon and Schuster, 1979.

INDEX